DEVOTIONS

from the KITCHEN TABLE

DEVOTIONS

from the KITCHEN TABLE

by STACY EDWARDS

THOMAS NELSON

Since 1798

Devotions from the Kitchen Table

© 2017 Thomas Nelson

Published in Nashville, Tennessee, by Thomas Nelson. Thomas Nelson is a registered trademark of HarperCollins Christian Publishing, Inc.

Interior Photos: Shutterstock

Thomas Nelson titles may be purchased in bulk for educational, business, fund-raising, or sales promotional use. For information, please e-mail SpecialMarkets@ThomasNelson.com.

Unless otherwise noted, Scripture quotations are taken from the Holy Bible, New International Version®, NIV®. Copyright © 1973, 1978, 1984, 2011 by Biblica, Inc.® Used by permission of Zondervan. All rights reserved worldwide. www.zondervan.com. The "NIV" and "New International Version" are trademarks registered in the United States Patent and Trademark Office by Biblica, Inc.®

Scripture quotations marked ESV are from the ESV® Bible (The Holy Bible, English Standard Version®). Copyright © 2001 by Crossway, a publishing ministry of Good News Publishers. Used by permission. All rights reserved.

Scripture quotations marked HCSB are from the Holman Christian Standard Bible®. Copyright © 1999, 2000, 2002, 2003, 2009 by Holman Bible Publishers. Used by permission. HCSB® is a federally registered trademark of Holman Bible Publishers.

Scripture quotations marked THE MESSAGE are from *The Message*. Copyright © by Eugene H. Peterson 1993, 1994, 1995, 1996, 2000, 2001, 2002. Used by permission of Tyndale House Publishers, Inc.

Scripture quotations marked NASB are from New American Standard Bible®. Copyright © 1960, 1962, 1963, 1968, 1971, 1972, 1973, 1975, 1977, 1995 by The Lockman Foundation. Used by permission. (www.Lockman.org)

Scripture quotations marked NLT are from the *Holy Bible*, New Living Translation. © 1996, 2004, 2007, 2013 by Tyndale House Foundation. Used by permission of Tyndale House Publishers, Inc., Carol Stream, Illinois 60188. All rights reserved.

Any Internet addresses, phone numbers, or company or product information printed in this book are offered as a resource and are not intended in any way to be or to imply an endorsement by Thomas Nelson, nor does Thomas Nelson vouch for the existence, content, or services of these sites, phone numbers, companies, or products beyond the life of this book.

ISBN-13: 978-0-7180-9187-3

Printed in China

16 17 18 19 20 TIMS 10 9 8 7 6 5 4 3 2 1

CONTENTS

GIVING THANKS

He took the seven loaves and the fish, and when he had given thanks, he broke
them and gave them to the disciples, and they in turn to the people.

MATTHEW 15:36

What rules do you have at your kitchen table? No elbows on the table, perhaps? Maybe electronics are a huge no-no at dinnertime. Or when you were a child, maybe nothing would elicit a warning glare from your parents quite like chewing with your mouth open.

In our house we don't have a rule so much as a rhyme, and it goes like this: "You get what you get, and you don't throw a fit." (In order to make this rhyme, use your best Southern twang.) Any child who says, "This is exactly what I hoped you would serve, Mom!" receives bonus points. The general idea is that we expect everyone to be grateful.

No parent expects children to love every food that ever touches their plates. But slaving over a stove in an attempt to nourish your little people only to have them grimace as if you had served dirt on a plate is disheartening. The truth is that we all are just looking for a little gratitude.

Matthew describes a scene where many people had gathered to hear Jesus teach and to receive healing. Four thousand men (plus women and children) surrounded Jesus, and they were hungry. The disciples looked at the small amount of available food and deemed it not enough for the crowd. Haven't we all looked at our resources, time, or abilities and thought, *What can God do with this?*

But Jesus took the loaves and fish in His hands, and He gave thanks for what was before Him. He was grateful for the little before Him because He knew that, with God, a little can be more than enough. God can take whatever we bring Him and use it in miraculous ways. It's what He does!

Gratitude is easy after God multiplies the loaves and fish—after the bill is paid, the job is offered, or the diagnosis is good. What if we chose, instead, to be grateful before that? What if we trusted God not to take what we have and make it more but to take what we have and use it as He sees fit? Let's be people who give thanks on the front end—before the miracle.

Thank You, Lord, for being such a faithful provider. Each day
You give me exactly what I need. Help me remember that,
with You, the little I have can become more than enough.

GRANDMA'S KITCHEN

Jesus Christ is the same yesterday and today and forever.

HEBREWS 13:8

Turn on any home-decorating show, and you'll see how easy it seems to redecorate your kitchen. If you get tired of the color on the walls, a gallon of paint can fix that. If the layout begins to bore you, just rearrange the furniture. You can take out a wall if your kitchen is too closed off and even add an island for more counter space. Anything is possible with a little imagination and elbow grease. Change is very "in" these days.

If your grandmother was like many, it's likely that her kitchen never changed. Maybe the table was always against the same wall just below the clock. The gigantic wooden fork and spoon hung above the mantel. The decorative owl magnets were always on the refrigerator. It was always exactly the same, right down to the weekly pill organizer on the windowsill. There is something very comforting about consistency.

We live in a world where things are constantly changing. People who praise you today may persecute you tomorrow. Jobs become obsolete. Loved ones pass away and friends move away. It's hard to keep your footing in a world that never stays the same. Aren't you glad our God never changes?

Jesus will always be who He has always been. He will always be found by those who seek Him. He will always be faithful and forgiving. His love for you will never fade, and His ability to save will never cease. The same Jesus who met the woman at the well sees you in your time of need. The same Jesus who conquered death for you can move the mountains that stand in your way.

Jesus is as close as your next breath. He is more faithful than your closest friend. He is trustworthy and true. Jesus is right where He has always been—even more than Grandma's kitchen.

Lord, I live in a constantly changing world, but I find great comfort in Your consistency. Thank You for always being who You have always been.

FIRST ONE AWAKE

*In the morning, L*ORD*, you hear my voice; in the morning*
I lay my requests before you and wait expectantly.

PSALM 5:3

It isn't easy to be the first one awake if you're not a morning person. You might be tempted to hit the snooze button a time or two. Perhaps your children serve as your alarm clock and your house is already in full motion when you arise. Or maybe you hit the floor running when you wake up.

On the other hand, there is something incredibly peaceful about rising early, being the first one awake, and sitting at the kitchen table with your Bible and a cup of hot coffee. You can enjoy a moment to take a deep breath, give yourself a pep talk, and meet with God before the busyness of the day begins.

Soon enough, the house will be filled with noise and activity. There will be doors slamming, people talking, and breakfasts being prepared. To awaken in the midst of the chaos can feel overwhelming. But in those early moments, while the rest of the house sleeps, it's just you and the God who loves you.

Having your quiet time with God in the morning isn't a biblical command. What works best may depend on the season of life you are in at the moment. For the longest time I would sit on the bathroom floor while my little ones bathed and have my time with the Lord. The *when* doesn't matter as much as being diligent in doing it at some point each day.

Still, if at all possible, you just can't beat meeting with God in the wee hours of the morn. David met with the Lord in the morning, laid his requests before Him, and then went about his day expecting to see God work. Don't we all want to see God move throughout our days? We can expect big things from a big God.

Let's rise early to meet with Him. He can fill our hearts with peace in those quiet moments before our days begin.

I love spending time with You, Lord, at any hour of the day, but there is something special about the wee hours of the morning. Thank You for always meeting me there.

SPECIAL DELIVERY

Carry each other's burdens, and in this way you will fulfill the law of Christ.

GALATIANS 6:2

Some days, dinnertime is a breeze. There are no wrecks on the commute home, the kids don't have any homework, and you are right on track with your meal plans for the week. You walk in the door to the smell of pot roast and potatoes in the slow cooker and throw together some homemade bread just because you can. Yes, some days you rock at this thing called life.

Then there are those other days. The commute home takes an extra thirty minutes, and you drove the last ten with your fuel light on. Your spouse is out of town, and your children inform you that they have a science project due the next day that they haven't started yet. You have no idea what it was you had planned to make for dinner with the pitiful offerings in your pantry. These are the days when the delivery person is your friend. It doesn't matter if the delivery is pizza, Chinese, or sandwiches—you just need someone to help shoulder the dinner burden.

During some seasons, life feels under control. Our kids are healthy, our marriages are happy, and our jobs are fulfilling. We're blessed with time for family vacations, date nights, and friends. Our social media posts are all beach photos and funny memes, and life is good.

Then there are those other seasons. We don't spend much time on social media because tears in the shower are not as pretty as toes in the sand. The car breaks down, the toilet overflows, and an unexpected bill comes in the mail. We feel disconnected from our spouse, and the kids are passing around a stomach bug. In those moments we need someone to come along and carry some of the burden.

The beauty of the body of Christ is that no one is meant to bear their burdens all alone. To fulfill the law of Christ is to come alongside another person, link arms, and take on some of the load. We are so much stronger together. Let's look around and see who is weakening under the weight of a burden, and let's carry it for them. It might be as simple as having dinner delivered to their door.

You knew that this life was too much for us to do alone, Lord.
Open my eyes to ways I can carry another person's burden.

FAMILY RECIPES

*After that whole generation had been gathered to their ancestors, another
generation grew up who knew neither the Lord nor what he had done for Israel.*

JUDGES 2:10

Everyone has that one recipe: Grandma Ruby used to make it, and then your mother made it, and now you've started making it for your children. It's written on an index card that has a butter stain. The ingredients include a dash of this and a pinch of that. The most important part of the recipe, however, is that it gets passed down to future generations. How else will people know that nutmeg is the secret ingredient in Aunt Audrey's Christmas cookies?

A whole generation of Israelites had seen the Lord do miraculous things. They had seen God deliver His people from slavery and sustain them in the wilderness. They had seen the Jordan River dry up, the walls of Jericho fall, and the sun stand still. Yet, when that generation passed away, the generation who followed did not have a relationship with the Lord or any knowledge of all He had done for Israel.

It has been said that "if we don't teach our children to follow Christ, the world will teach them not to." While the source of the sentiment is unknown, the truth of it is undeniable. We are responsible for passing our faith on to the generations that follow us. They need to know what we have seen the Lord do in our day.

What prayers has He answered? What blessings has He bestowed? Write it down. Others need to know. What do we know to be true of Him? What has He meant to us in the dark seasons of life?

May it not be said that the generation following us did not know what the Lord did for us.

Remind me, Lord, to recite Your wonders to the next generation.
May they know how mighty You have been in my day.

THE LAST PIECE OF PIE

"Commission Joshua, and encourage and strengthen him, for he will lead this
people across and will cause them to inherit the land that you will see."

DEUTERONOMY 3:28

It's hard not to be bitter when someone takes the last piece of pie. You hide it in the back of the refrigerator while you go about the nightly tasks of washing the dishes, bathing the children, and getting everyone ready for bed. You practically skip into the kitchen thinking of the slice of deliciousness that awaits you. You round the corner and gasp as you see your spouse finishing the last bite of the dessert you have been thinking about all evening.

Maybe something other than a piece of pie tempts you toward bitterness. Perhaps another person was offered the job that you had your heart set on. Someone else received the proposal that you have been dreaming of for the longest time. How do you feel when you see someone receive something that has been the desire of your heart? Satan would love for you to give in to bitterness and envy.

Moses had spent a lot of time preparing God's people for their entrance into the promised land. He had endured a lot of griping and spent quite a bit of time intervening on their behalf. In the end Moses disobeyed God, and the consequence was a big one. God forbade him from entering the promised land. More than that, God told Moses to encourage Joshua to do the very thing that Moses himself desired to do.

Deuteronomy 3:28 holds the key to battling bitterness. Encouragement conquers envy. We can begin to see situations differently when we take the focus off ourselves and look for ways to strengthen the other person. Let's learn to say, "Yay, you," instead of "Poor me." We can be happy for someone even if they get what we have been waiting on.

Even when it comes—heaven forbid—to the last piece of pie.

Teach me to encourage someone when I'm tempted to envy them, Lord. Let no root of bitterness grow in my heart. Help me point others to You.

CONTAINER GARDENING

I pray that the sharing of your faith may become effective for the full knowledge of every good thing that is in us for the sake of Christ.

PHILEMON V. 6 ESV

Container gardening is all the rage for people without the space to plant a proper garden or the time to invest in maintaining one. By planting a few items in pots on your porch or windowsill, you realize it isn't as hard as you imagined. You might be tempted to think that your little container garden wouldn't be worth the time (and wouldn't produce enough anyway), but the truth is that container gardening can be extremely effective.

Perhaps you viewed other gardens, and they seemed to require more time, effort, or knowledge than you were able to put into gardening. If you'll just try some container gardening, you'll find that your gardening method doesn't have to be complex in order to enjoy sweet basil. You can use what you have at your disposal and get the same result.

Basil is an herb that grows fast and with minimal effort. Basil may not be one of the first things you envision yourself growing, and you might think you'd have no need of it. But once you have fresh basil at your disposal, you begin seeing a need for it everywhere!

Sharing your faith is a bit like starting a container garden. Maybe you don't feel you have the knowledge, the boldness, or the time to engage someone on a spiritual level. You might even think there are no opportunities to share if your only "field" of influence is with other believers. But your way of sharing doesn't have to compare to anyone else's.

If we would ask God to open our eyes so we truly see the people around us, we would begin seeing countless needs. There are opportunities everywhere to share our faith with individuals who need to hear our story. We would begin to realize that the cashier who checks us out every Friday needs us to notice and encourage her. The neighbor to whom we wave but never speak is desperate for changes only Christ can bring.

You may think sharing your testimony is pointless, but once you make up your mind to do so, you will begin seeing a need for it everywhere.

Help me ignore the lies of the Enemy when he tells me that my little testimony could never be enough. Open my eyes, Lord, to those who need to hear my story.

A GENEROUS HELPING

Out of his fullness we have all received grace in place of grace already given.

JOHN 1:16

Certain situations make cause cooks to serve generous helpings. When you know that a person will love the dish you've made, that someone is in need of the meal you've made, or that you have more food than anyone could ever eat—well, you pile that plate high.

On the other hand, portions tend to be smaller when someone requests a second helping. After all, you want to be sure everyone has had their fair share and there's enough to go around.

Whether you have lots of growing kids to feed, a limited budget, or a teenage boy, seconds aren't always guaranteed. If you serve something particularly yummy for dinner, you'd best not take your eyes off your plate because someone might snatch a biscuit out from under your nose. It's every woman for herself when bread is involved.

When Jesus dishes out grace, He serves it up like a hot, creamy dish of Mama's macaroni and cheese. It's a generous helping every time. He doesn't skimp when you ask for seconds. He doesn't make you wait until everyone has had some before you can have more. Best of all, Jesus never runs out of what you need. He isn't scraping the pot, hoping there's enough. He offers the same measure of grace each time, and it is a full measure.

Have you fallen into the same pit again? Do you fear there isn't enough grace to cover you this time? If so, you're wrong. Jesus' supply is limitless, and He is generous with it. When John described the grace of Jesus, he said that we receive "grace in place of grace already given." The grace given the second, third, or fourth time is just as generous as His first serving.

Lord, I crave Your grace more than any serving of comfort food.
Thank You for Your generous helpings that will never run out.

AFRAID OF THE DARK

The people stood far off, while Moses drew near to the thick darkness where God was.

EXODUS 20:21 ESV

How comfortable are you in the dark? Is it calming or creepy? Do you feel perfectly secure, or are you guilty of mistaking the bathrobe hanging on the door for an intruder? Do you buy nightlights, pretend they're for your children, then plug them in your bedroom? Nyctophobia, or fear of the dark, is a real thing, and lots of people have it.

Has fear ever kept you from meeting with God? Many sermons about hearing God's voice have been preached from 1 Kings 19:11–13. This passage talks about God being in a whisper rather than in the strong wind, earthquake, or fire. It's true that we do, sometimes, look for a big production from God and miss His still, small voice. We think we would prefer Him to be a little louder, but how do we respond when He does come in thunder and lightning? We like the idea of a gentle whisper, but are we still eager to draw near when there is a smoking mountain and a thick darkness? What happens when fear fills the space between where God stands and where we stand?

The children of Israel stood far off, away from the thick darkness. They felt safer in the light even though the light was farther away from God.

As people of God, we must draw near to Him wherever He may be. When God is calling us into a place that seems dark and scary, we cannot stand far off in fear. We must, like Moses, embrace the thick darkness if that is where we find Him. If we will trust God enough to draw near, we will find that even the darkness is not dark when we are with Him (Psalm 139:12).

*I don't have to be afraid when I'm with You, Lord,
because there is no darkness in Your presence.*

CRUMBS UNDER THE TABLE

As it is written: "There is no one righteous, not even one."

ROMANS 3:10

When preparing our home for guests, some of us are content to hide some clutter, close a few doors, and light a candle. Then there are those of us who spend days cleaning every nook and cranny of our homes. We exhaust ourselves trying to present a perfectly tidy and organized home to people who simply want to enjoy our company.

One pastor's wife learned this lesson while preparing her home for a visit from some church members. She wanted everything to be perfect and was slightly stressed until a dear friend gave some great counsel: "No one can relate to seemingly perfect people. Leave some crumbs under the kitchen table." The advice made perfect sense. We aren't drawn to relationships with people who seem to have it all together. We gravitate toward people who are genuine. We don't need advice as much as we need someone to say, "Me too."

Presenting a certain image to those around us is tempting. We take pride in multitasking and smile when people ask how we are able to do it all. We sit in pews with our best clothes, our Sunday smiles, and our children all in a row. No one knows that our hearts are heavy and the days are hard. We isolate ourselves in an attempt to impress others, and everyone loses when we do that.

Someone needs us to admit that we're having a hard time navigating motherhood so that she can say, "Me too." Someone out there longs for a friend to confess that she thought her life would look different so she can say, "I did too." Let's be our true selves and give others permission to do the same.

None of us has it all together. Scripture reminds us that none of us is righteous on our own. We all struggle with sin of some kind, have seasons of doubt, and need forgiveness on a regular basis. It's okay to let people see the occasional struggle, failing, or crumb under the kitchen table. Acknowledging our imperfections is a great opportunity to point them to the perfect Savior.

Pretending to be perfect adds stress to me and takes glory away from You, Lord. Thank You for the gift of genuine relationships.

SEASONED WITH SALT

Your speech should always be gracious, seasoned with salt, so that
you may know how you should answer each person.

COLOSSIANS 4:6 HCSB

Seasoning is vital to any dish you make. Steak, pasta, or seafood all need the appropriate mix of spices to wow a person's palate. One thing that can cause any dish to be a disappointment is for it to not have enough salt. Watch any cooking show and you'll see that cooks salt everything from pasta water to ground beef to salads. Salt makes rice pop and adds an extra dose of pizzazz to spaghetti sauce. It's an appropriate addition to almost any dish and can be found on practically every table in every restaurant. You just can't go wrong with a dash of salt.

In the book of Colossians, Paul taught the Christ-followers to season their conversations with salt. First, he told them to make the best use of their time. In other words, share the gospel at every opportunity. Paul then went on to tell them to always be gracious in their conversations. Grace in a conversation is like salt in a dish; you can't go wrong.

Have you ever eaten a particular dish at someone's home and been surprised that you liked it? Maybe brussels sprouts have always triggered your gag reflex. Then Nana serves them one day for Sunday brunch, so you try them to be polite and discover that they're quite tasty! It's because they are seasoned in a way that makes them more palatable.

Our conversations with others should be the same way. We don't always know people's experiences. They may have had an encounter where the gospel was presented in an aggressive or harsh way or may have a past that causes them to be hesitant to listen. Our conversations should always be well seasoned, and a dash of grace is always appropriate.

Lord, remind me to always season my speech with grace. Teach me to speak the truth, but to speak it in love. May every word that comes out of my mouth point others to You.

AN UNEXPECTED GIFT

Israel said to Joseph, "I never expected to see your face; and
behold, God has let me see your offspring also."

GENESIS 48:11 ESV

Have you ever had something you wanted so desperately, but you tried to not hope for it so that you wouldn't be disappointed? Maybe it was a certain toy when you were little, a car when you turned sixteen, or an engagement ring on Valentine's Day. We do that, don't we? We try to not get our hopes up in an effort to guard our hearts.

As far as Israel knew, his son had been dead for years. He had no reason to expect to see Joseph's face again on earth. It would have never occurred to him to hope for a surprise reunion. Who would even ask for such a thing? Isn't that just like God to go above and beyond? Not only did Israel get to see his son's face again, but he was also able to see his grandchildren as well!

Has something amazing ever happened to you or someone you love and you thought, *I never expected* . . . ? We've all had moments like that, and it makes us wonder what other mysteries we may have missed out on. After all, Jesus says that we have not because we ask not (James 4:2), so what other things have we failed to ask for because we just don't expect them to happen?

Our longings often come from a tender place within us, and we fear the damage another disappointment may bring. Who knows what could happen if we didn't worry about disappointments but were, instead, bold in our requests, as we have permission to be (Hebrews 4:16)?

Let's open our hearts to what God wants to do in our lives. Then we'll be able to say, "I never expected and, behold, God . . ."

Why do I limit Your love for me, Lord? Give me the
boldness to approach Your throne in my time of need.

FAMILY REUNION

*Remember that at that time you were separate from Christ, excluded
from citizenship in Israel and foreigners to the covenants of the
promise, without hope and without God in the world.*

Ephesians 2:12

Many of us have traveled far from where we were born. We have visited places, interacted with people, and had experiences that helped mold us into the people we are today. It can be exciting to visit new places and see new things. It's also important to remember where our roots were first planted.

A family reunion is a special time when you have the opportunity to go back to familiar places and see familiar faces. Reunions offer the chance to be reunited with the people who know you better than you know yourself. They've seen you fail and try again, fall and get back up, make mistakes and learn from them. Going back often serves as a reminder that you did not get where you are on your own.

Satan would love nothing more than for us to take all the credit for getting to where we are today. If we achieve any manner of success, he wants us to pat ourselves on the back. If we receive any accolades, he desires us to take pride in them. The problem is when we take all of the credit for our gifts and accomplishments, God does not receive any of the glory. Paul warned believers that it's vital to remember where we were before God intervened.

Prior to trusting Christ for salvation, we were "without hope and without God." Can you recall what it felt like to be hopeless? The vast difference between attending the funeral of someone who believed versus someone who did not is hope. If you've been a believer for a significant length of time, it's easy to take that hope for granted. Paul told us to remember. Living in those memories for too long is unpleasant, but remembering helps us appreciate where we are now and what Christ has done for us.

When we're tempted to take credit for our successes or to take hope for granted, let's remember what life was like and where we would be without Christ.

Thank You for how far You've brought me, Lord. Help me remember where I would be without You.

SUPPER'S ON

"If I go and prepare a place for you, I will come again and will take you to myself, that where I am you may be also."

JOHN 14:3 ESV

At several points during the day, children will ask, "When is dinner?" Some days are full of activities, and dinnertime can sneak up. Then there are other days when folks are hungry (and maybe a little grumpy) and dinnertime seems very far away. Emotions are a little more extreme when hunger is involved.

One solution for keeping your people calm is to just heat a little oil in a cast iron skillet and throw in some diced onions. Nothing sounds or smells more divine than some onions sautéing in a pan. The sizzle and the aroma lets hungry bellies know that something good is coming their way. They don't have to know exactly what it is or even when it will arrive. They just need to know that something is in the works, and it'll be worth the wait.

We've all had those days when we long for Christ's return. We open our eyes and immediately wish for the end of the day. Have you ever found yourself asking, *When are You coming back, Lord?* If so, you know the feeling well. Heaven just seems very far away. Hardships are overwhelming and heartaches ever present. Some days go quickly, but the ones that don't *really* don't.

The good news for those of us awaiting Christ's return is there's a way to keep ourselves calm on the craziest of days while also reminding ourselves that Jesus is, in fact, coming. We just need to be in His Word! Over and over, Jesus reminded His people that He was coming back. He told us in John 14 that He's preparing a place for us. We can go to the book of Revelation and get ourselves a little glimpse of heaven. We can study Scripture and remind ourselves that something good is on the way for those of us who believe. We don't have to know exactly what it will look like or even when it will take place. We can rest easy knowing that something is in the works, and it'll be worth the wait.

I have a hunger, Lord, that will not be satisfied until I stand in Your presence. Help me live and love faithfully until that day.

HOME REPAIRS

"Be on guard, so that your hearts will not be weighted down with
dissipation and drunkenness and the worries of life."

LUKE 21:34 NASB

How stressful is it when something breaks around the house? Doesn't everything just seem a tad worse when the furnace goes kaput, the refrigerator quits refrigerating, or the kitchen sink won't drain?

No one has to tell you that things could be worse, and you don't need to be reminded about all the people who are struggling with much bigger things. In the grand scheme of things, these are simply inconveniences. But the truth is that those annoyances can be the final straw when you are the one washing your dishes in a bucket.

In the little anxieties of life, we can find Satan hard at work. The huge issues don't necessarily take us out. We can rally for the big things. We will trust God for miracles. But those little things can be like death by a thousand cuts. They can become a distraction the Enemy will use to his advantage.

The Enemy knows we're going to take those big things straight to God. He knows that when tragedy strikes, we'll fall on our faces before our God. But when the car breaks down, the toilet overflows, the kids lose the library books, or an unexpected bill arrives—how distracted from the things of Christ are we at that point?

The next time we feel overwhelmed or heavyhearted over the day-to-day worries of this life, let's remind ourselves that these annoyances are Satan's pathetic attempt to distract us. Let's decide, on the front end, that we will not allow it to work.

Teach me to see beyond the daily worries of this life,
Lord. When the Enemy wants to keep me distracted,
help me stay focused on things above.

IN REAL LIFE

Though I have much to write to you, I would rather not use paper and ink. Instead
I hope to come to you and talk face to face, so that our joy may be complete.

2 John v. 12 esv

We live in a time when we call individuals we've never met "friends," and we can live vicariously through other people's posts and photos. Something exciting takes place, and we're quick to document it online so our friends and family can know what's happening in our lives. We have hundreds of folks who will "like" our funny comments and share our inspirational posts but are nowhere to be found when our hearts are broken or our babies are sick. We need some IRL friends.

IRL is an acronym for *in real life*. The need to differentiate exists because so many of us live online lives and talk about complete strangers as if they were childhood friends. We share way too much with people who aren't invested in our lives. If you've ever read someone's post on social media and thought, *That woman needs a diary*, then you know what we're talking about here. It's okay for some things, good or bad, to take place in our lives and not be shared with the masses. Some things were meant to be shared face-to-face, in real life, over a cup of coffee.

When John wrote 2 John, he wanted to share exciting things to which paper and ink wouldn't do justice. Paper and ink would have been the modern technology of his day, something akin to texting for us perhaps. It probably would have been great to read the news in a letter from John, but to hear it face-to-face would result in complete joy.

Let's go back to the days when, if we had some great news to tell, our first thought was, *I can't wait to see her face when she finds out!* No emoji can take the place of some face-to-face, in-real-life, complete joy.

Let me not trade in-real-life friends for virtual ones, Lord. Thank
You for the face-to-face friends You have placed in my life.

MEAL TRAIN

And many others . . . were supporting them from their possessions.

Luke 8:3 hcsb

The meal train has been around for generations. When someone has a major life event take place, someone will rally the troops and begin coordinating meals for that person and his or her family. While we may not be able to take away someone's pain or problem, it *is* possible to take away the "What's for dinner?" dilemma. Serving others isn't a cure-all; it's a way to come alongside another person.

If you've ever had the blessing of being the beneficiary of a meal train, you're aware that the offerings can vary tremendously. One family may drop off a "meat and three," and another may have pizza delivered to your door. One friend may have the time to make something from scratch while someone else may purchase items premade. People give based on the time and money available to them, and one is not better or worse than the other.

The art of the meal train has changed over the years. A gift card may take the place of a pound cake, but the spirit remains the same. We use whatever we have at our disposal to love on those in our homes, churches, and communities. There is no right or wrong way to do it.

Many people followed Jesus throughout His earthly ministry. The gospel of Luke mentions several women who were known to be supporters of Christ's work. Among those listed in chapter 8 are a single woman and a married woman. There are some who would have been considered women of means and others who weren't able to give quite as much.

The beauty of ministry is that it has nothing to do with how much someone gives and everything to do with a person's heart. Christ was not more impressed with Joanna because she was married and, most likely, more financially stable.

Scripture says that the women gave "from their possessions." Generosity is giving from what you have been given. We can all do that.

We don't have to worry about what others are or are not giving. Let's learn to support and serve one another from our possessions just like the women did in Jesus' day. If we have a heart to love like Jesus loves, we have what it takes to be generous. We just need to keep the train moving.

Teach me to be a cheerful giver, Lord. Open my eyes to opportunities to use what You've given me to bless others.

SECURITY CODE

We have this hope as an anchor for the soul, firm and secure.
It enters the inner sanctuary behind the curtain.

Gone are the days when people could sleep with their windows open or their doors unlocked. Everything is secured. We have security codes for our computers, our cell phones, and our garage doors, and we all get to pick our own codes. If you ever need to give someone your security code, it's important that you really trust that person.

It's also important that the person receiving the code understands what they've been given access to in order to avoid any embarrassing situations. My dad could tell you more about this. He was supposed to stop by someone's garage to pick up some books, and it was a home he had never visited. He set out with the address and the garage's access code.

Once in the garage, he couldn't find the books anywhere. He called the individual to explain that the books were not there but that the sports car in the garage was quite nice. My dad was quickly informed that he was in the wrong garage! It turned out that two neighbors had the exact same passcode to their homes, and he had entered the wrong one.

In biblical times a believer could go only so far when entering the temple. The inner sanctuary was off-limits; the ordinary believer simply didn't have access to certain areas. Then Jesus came and gave us access behind the curtain, which brought hope.

There are many who try to make up their own security code to salvation, but Jesus really is the only One who opens the way to eternal life. Because of what Christ has done, we have access to the Father (Ephesians 2:18). As if that wasn't exciting enough, we can share the security code with everyone we come in contact with! Let's not keep the truth all to ourselves. We can make sure those we love know the code and understand exactly what it allows them to access.

I'm so grateful that it's not a guessing game with You, Lord. Thank You for the access You provided through Your death on the cross.

FIRST DISH

"You have forsaken the love you had at first."

REVELATION 2:4

What's the first meal you learned to make? Perhaps it was spaghetti, sloppy joes, or some sort of casserole. Did you feel like you were invincible the first time you made a successful dish? We're usually pretty proud of those first culinary creations, and we tend to serve them pretty consistently. Maybe you had ramen noodles your entire freshman year of college or served your new husband sweet potato casserole for a sweet forever.

Those meals seem positively delightful when we're basking in the "look what I can do" glow. But how do they seem several years later? If someone served you a bowl of ramen noodles today, would you give a sentimental smile or would you have to pass?

In the book of Revelation, God gave His assessment of seven churches, letting them know what they had been doing well and what areas needed improvement. He had many good things to point out regarding the church in Ephesus. They exhibited great patience, discernment, and endurance. Yet God warned them to be careful regarding one aspect of their ministry: they no longer had the love they had at first.

They were doing all the right things. They were pressing on but without passion. They had lost the love. It's easy to do, isn't it? Don't we do the very same thing in various areas of our lives? We find ourselves doing the tasks associated with our roles as spouse or parent or caretaker or employee but without any of the joy that once fueled us. We do things out of obligation instead of desire. We eat the sloppy joes just to ease the hunger, forgetting that we once craved them.

If we aren't careful, this temptation to grow cold can creep into our relationship with Jesus. We still pray but with a little less passion. We still study Scripture but with a little less enthusiasm. We serve others but with a little less love.

Let's be intentional about keeping the spark alive and, if we need to, reclaim the love we had at first. We shouldn't forget what it was like before God intervened. Even if we have been believers for decades, let's ask God to give us the passion that we felt when the love was new.

Forgive me, Lord, for the times when I make You just another item on my to-do list. Ignite a fire in my soul for You.

PINWHEELS

For we are His creation, created in Christ Jesus for good works,
which God prepared ahead of time so that we should walk in them.

EPHESIANS 2:10 HCSB

The pinwheel is one of the prettiest things to ever grace a flower pot or herb garden. They're a dime a dozen, and they aren't particularly fancy. They come in an array of colors and designs, but they all have one thing in common: in order for them to do what they were created to do, a breeze must blow.

Although they're pretty enough when motionless, pinwheels were created for much more. When the wind blows, the pinwheels spin, and the colors are on full display, shining in the sun. Then the true beauty of the pinwheel is evident.

When God was planning out His creation, man was the best thing to grace His garden. He looked at all of the good things and added something *very* good (Genesis 1:31). God created people in a beautiful array of colors, talents, and personalities. We are all different, but we have one thing in common: if we are to do all that we were created to do, we need the breath of God.

We're all created with a purpose and a desire to live lives that matter. We just need to be sensitive to the nudging of the Holy Spirit. We may look fragile to onlookers, and we may even feel fragile. But when the breath of God blows and we begin doing what we were meant to do, that's when our beauty and strength are on full display.

It doesn't matter what the world throws at us or how hard it hits us; we will not be shaken or made to run. We only move when God gives the word. And when He does, we'll show our true colors and reflect His love and grace onto those around us.

Let's embrace the wind, wildly spinning and shining for Him.

I'm tempted to live in fear because I'm all too aware of my own fragility and failings. But I long to do what You created me to do, Lord. Help me to reflect You.

A CHICKEN IN EVERY POT

You ask and do not receive, because you ask wrongly, to spend it on your passions.

JAMES 4:3 ESV

A lot of promises are made during political campaigns. Candidates will often say whatever they believe the voters want to hear. This is what happened in 1928 when Herbert Hoover ran under the slogan "A chicken in every pot and a car in every garage." To sway voters, Hoover promised financial prosperity for the country. As it turned out, voting with a motive of monetary reward didn't achieve the results people wanted. The stock market crashed the following year, and the Great Depression began.

The result is much the same when we ask things of God with selfish motives. Jesus taught His followers, "Ask and it will be given to you" (Matthew 7:7). Why, then, were some people in New Testament times asking and not receiving (James 4:3)? *The Message* explains it this way: "You're spoiled children, each wanting your own way." Anything we ask of the Lord should have the ultimate goal of His glorification.

The Lord's Prayer, found in Matthew 6:9–13, instructs us to pray for things that would glorify God and grow His kingdom. It teaches us to ask for His protection as we do His work and for defeat of His enemies.

God hears all our prayers, but He does not say yes to those that only serve to satisfy selfish desires. He honors those that come from a pure heart and a desire to honor Him. God is good, and all His ways are perfect (Psalm 18:30). We can trust Him to honor these God-focused prayers and protect us from misguided ones.

If we're ever in doubt, we can ask ourselves, *Why am I desiring this, and who stands to benefit from it?* If we are honest with the answers, we will know whether we can expect to receive the thing for which we ask.

What I think is best doesn't always line up with Your plan, Lord. Examine my heart and only grant those requests that will glorify Your name.

ROOM AT THE TABLE

Being found in appearance as a man, he humbled himself by
becoming obedient to death—even death on a cross!

PHILIPPIANS 2:8

There is something special about gathering around a kitchen table. Imagine a large family including five children and a set of grandparents—the sort of household that would typically own a long farm table or spacious kitchen island. But what if the dining area is cramped, with room enough for only a small table designed for four? Will that family of nine relegate certain members to another room? No, they'll improvise by dragging chairs from around the house into the kitchen, squeezing tight, sharing seats, and bumping elbows. There's always room for one more at the table.

Have you ever stopped to think about the people who witnessed the crucifixion of Christ? The centurion was there (Matthew 27:54). Followers and scoffers. Passersby and gawkers. Luke said "all [Jesus'] acquaintances" were part of the group (23:49 ESV). There was, no doubt, some bumping of elbows in the crowd.

Consider the old hymn "Room at the Cross for You." That is the beauty of Christ's sacrifice. The beauty of the cross is that it was for everyone. The woman at the well was just as welcome as the mother of Christ. There was room for those who came to mock but left believing. There was room for those who doubted and those who denied. The cross was for one and all, and it still is today.

There is room for the one who grew up in church. There is room for the one who has never stepped foot inside a church. It doesn't matter what you have done because the blood of Christ covered it all. There's room at the cross for you.

Thank You, Lord, that no matter how many have
come before me, Your grace never runs out.

FREEZER COOKING

If your law had not been my delight, I would have perished in my affliction.

PSALM 119:92

Freezer cooking can be a huge time saver and stress reducer for those leading busy lives. The idea is that you take one day or weekend and cook multiple meals that you then place in the freezer.

Freezer cooking can work a number of ways. You can make a month's worth of meals and then not cook for thirty days. That would be amazing, right? The downside is that, eventually, your freezer is once again empty, and another marathon cooking session is necessary to replenish it. Therefore, some people prefer to fill the freezer with good meals and then use the meals sporadically while continuing to add to the stash.

When utilized this way, the freezer is never empty, and you are never left without dinner after a busy day. **But** you know that if you make only thirty meals and then consume thirty meals, day thirty-one will be a doozy for sure. It's just the way it works. What you want, instead, is to always have something in the freezer that you can pull out on a tough day.

Reading God's Word is a lot like freezer cooking. There are seasons when we have the time and energy to do marathon studying sessions. Times like this are beneficial, meaningful, and wonderful, but we can't stop there. The knowledge of and intimacy with God will sustain us for a while, but if we don't continually replenish our hearts and minds, we won't have anything to pull from on a tough day.

When time allows for in-depth study, go for it! Then on all the other days, continue spending time reading Scripture, and let God continue to fill your heart and mind with good things. You can keep your "freezer" full in multiple ways: by praying continually, following a Scripture reading plan, interacting with godly people, and listening to music that glorifies God.

Then on those days when you're feeling low, you can pull from the overflow of your heart and meditate on good things the Holy Spirit has revealed to you.

Too many times, I walk out into the world hungry, Lord.
Your Word says that You fill the hungry with good
things, and my heart's desire is to be filled by You.

YOU ALL, Y'ALL,
AND YOU GUYS

*No foul language is to come from your mouth, but only what is good for
building up someone in need, so that it gives grace to those who hear.*

EPHESIANS 4:29 HCSB

If you've lived in multiple states over the years, you know it's possible to adjust and blend in pretty much anywhere. You can dress like the locals, have the same interests as the locals, and drink your coffee where the locals drink coffee. You can appear as if you have always lived in that very community—until you open your mouth.

A Harvard linguistics project attempted to determine where a person was from based on their word choices. *Do you drink* soda *or* pop? *Do you water your lawn with a* garden hose *or a* hosepipe? *Have you ever told someone that you were going to* red up *a room?* You may be able to blend in anywhere for a short time, but how you speak and the words you use will have folks asking, "You're not from around here, are you?"

Paul made it clear in his letter to the Ephesians that how we speak matters. If we are Christ's disciples, then the way we talk will show that. There are instructions throughout Scripture specifically addressing how we are to communicate with people: No foul language (Ephesians 4:29). Our words should not be rash or impulsive (Proverbs 12:18). We shouldn't gossip (Proverbs 20:19) or tell lies (Psalm 34:13).

We may look the part of a believer and do the same things as a believer, but if our heart isn't right, our words will give us away. Like the psalmist, we want our words to be acceptable in God's sight (Psalm 19:14). People should know, when they speak to us, that we are a part of the body of Christ.

Lord, guard my lips so that every word points others to You.

SLEEP LIKE A BABY

Gideon came to the Jordan and crossed over, he and the 300
men who were with him, exhausted yet pursuing.

JUDGES 8:4 ESV

Whoever coined the phrase "sleep like a baby" clearly never had one wake them up every two hours for nights on end. Having a newborn in your home makes you understand all those tired moms on social media. You begin to realize that coffee is a necessity and showering is a luxury. Words like *sleep, tired,* and *drained* do not seem to do justice to how you feel.

A new baby in the house brings absolute exhaustion but also the ability to keep going. A God-given endurance seems to accompany the bone weariness, enabling a new mom or dad to be exhausted yet continue to do the things that need to be done. Whether it's taking care of a newborn or an ailing parent, working extra hours to make ends meet, or trying to get through the day, life can be exhausting.

Gideon knew a thing or two about physical exhaustion. He and his men had been engaged in battle, and Gideon himself described his troops as "worn out" (Judges 8:5). Gideon had overcome a great amount of fear and, in obedience to God's commands, set out to conquer the very enemy he had been hiding from when God came to him. Once Gideon chose to be a part of what God was doing, there was no stopping him.

Sometimes, perhaps even often, God will call us to do hard things. At times we'll be physically and emotionally weary. We must decide on the front end that, even in our exhaustion, we'll continue to pursue the will of God.

There's no shame in being tired. We can know that God gives strength to the weary and power to the weak (Isaiah 40:29). We can also know that if we'll continue pursuing Him, we'll reap the reward of those who don't give up (Galatians 6:9).

There are times when I grow weary, Lord. In those moments,
give me the strength I need to continue pursuing You so
I can be counted among those who didn't give up.

CHERRY DUMP CAKE

It is by grace you have been saved, through faith—and
this is not from yourselves, it is the gift of God.

EPHESIANS 2:8

Have you ever made a really simple dish and then someone asked you for the recipe? It can be a little awkward. Do the instructions "mix all ingredients together" constitute a recipe? What about "dump everything in a slow cooker and walk away"? We're often tempted to think that things need to be complicated in order to be impressive.

One of the best desserts to take to a gathering is a cherry dump cake, which is made, as the name might suggest, by dumping the ingredients into a dish and baking. For the longest time, I would refer to it as a "cherry-pineapple dessert" to make it sound like more work was involved. I would almost take pride in people assuming it involved a lot of effort on my part. Here's the thing, though: when folks thought it was difficult, no one wanted to make it.

Sometimes we make following Jesus appear complicated. We give people a long list of dos and don'ts. We show off our good works as if they were ingredients in the recipe of salvation. We even convince ourselves that we must do X, Y, and Z in order to be right with God. Without even realizing it, we make salvation seem too much to even hope for.

But salvation is a gift. You couldn't earn it if you wanted to, and you could never afford it even if it were for sale. It isn't complicated, and you don't need any special skills. The recipe is the same for you as it was for the jailer in Acts 16:30–31. You just need to believe in Jesus and you'll be saved.

Jesus did not make it complicated to come to Him. You simply come. It's as easy as throwing together a cherry dump cake.

Thank You, Lord, for the uncomplicated truth of the gospel. You've made it so that anyone can comprehend Your Word and come into Your presence.

WASHING DISHES

When Jesus heard it, he said to them, "Those who are well have no need of a physician, but those who are sick. I came not to call the righteous, but sinners."

MARK 2:17 ESV

There are two types of people when it comes to using a dishwasher. Some will take all the dishes straight from the stove and dinner table, give them a quick shake over the trash can, put them in the machine, and hope for the best. (If you've ever wondered how many times you should leave that pot in the dishwasher before giving up and hand washing it, the answer is always "one more time.")

Then there are the ones who prewash their dishes. They'll rinse each dish, ensure there is no visible evidence the dish was ever used, and then methodically load each piece into the dishwasher. Cups go on top, plates all face the same direction on the bottom, and forks are placed with prongs facing up. It's hard to give the machine too much credit when so much of the work is already done.

Many people struggle with coming to Christ because they feel unclean and unworthy. They think they must clean themselves up before approaching the throne of grace. The problem with that is that we could never prewash ourselves enough to be worthy. He came so we wouldn't waste our lives trying.

Jesus spent His days showing grace to a woman who had five husbands and was living with a man who was not her husband (John 4:3–30); stopping in the midst of a crowd to speak to a woman who had been bleeding for twelve years (Matthew 9:20–22); and calling out to a tax collector up in a tree and inviting Himself to dinner (Luke 19:1–10). Christ came to make us clean because we could never do it ourselves.

Nothing could ever clean us like the blood of Jesus has already done.

Forgive me for the times I've tried to clean myself, Lord. Thank You for Your precious blood that washed me and made me new.

SLOWING DOWN

When He heard that [Lazarus] was sick, He stayed two
more days in the place where He was.

JOHN 11:6 HCSB

Do you ever catch yourself hurrying for no apparent reason? Why do we do that? Many of us repeatedly find ourselves rushing to do one more load of laundry, run a quick errand, or finish one more task before the end of the day. We know the world isn't going to stop if dinner isn't ready at 6:00 sharp or if that e-mail isn't answered until the next day, but we still feel the pressure to move quicker and finish sooner. When did we decide that hurrying was necessary?

I, for one, don't have a single memory of my grandparents rushing anywhere. Anything that needed to be taken care of could happen in between cups of coffee, chats with friends, and episodes of TV game shows. Wouldn't they shake their heads at the way the world has gotten into such a hurry?

Jesus certainly didn't hurry through His days. He was on His way to a sick twelve-year-old girl when the bleeding woman was able to reach through the crowd and touch Him. Not only was Jesus moving slowly enough for her to touch Him, but He also took the time to stop and speak to her. Jesus was more concerned with healing a heart than hurrying on to the next thing.

When word reached Jesus that His friend Lazarus was sick, Jesus stayed where He was for two more days. We're not told what took place in those two days, but we can safely assume that sins were forgiven, people were healed, and lives were changed because that's what Jesus did, and He didn't rush through it.

Jesus didn't hurry past hurting people. He didn't rush from activity to activity, obligation to obligation, or place to place. He cared about people enough to slow down. Let's do the same. Let's take a deep breath, look around us, and see the people we have been hurrying by.

I don't want to hurry anymore, Lord. Help me slow down and see the hurting people You have placed around me.

TASTE BUDS CHANGE

Be joyful in hope, patient in affliction, faithful in prayer.

ROMANS 12:12

What is your least favorite food? Liver, perhaps? Green olives? For me, it was always tomatoes. The smell alone—mercy! Up until a few months ago, I would have listed tomatoes as my least favorite food of all time.

My Grandma Wike gave me some words of wisdom in her day. For instance, she would insist that biting my fingernails would give me worms. I'm pretty sure that she totally made that one up, and also, I am still a nail biter. (Sorry, Grandma.) The other nugget of wisdom I still remember clearly is that, according to her, a person's taste buds change every seven years.

Maybe she read it in a magazine. Perhaps it was something her mother told her in an effort to get her to eat green peas. Of course, it's also possible that Grandma completely made it up. All I know is that for the past thirty years, I have felt obligated to occasionally try tomatoes.

Then it happened: one random afternoon, I ate a tomato and liked it. I guess Grandma was right; taste buds change, and you should never give up on any food.

Chances are that you've been praying for some person for a long time. There is probably someone you long to see healed, saved, or granted a long-awaited desire. You've prayed and pleaded and wondered, *How long?*

Don't give up. Do not listen to the Enemy when he whispers defeat in your ears. Keep bringing your loved ones before Jesus in prayer. Think of the men who brought their friend to Jesus for healing in Mark 2. They weren't put off by the effort it would take to reach Christ. They climbed onto the roof! They dug until they had created an opening, and they lowered their friend to Jesus.

It's not too late. Your prayers are being heard, and people are worth the effort. Keep praying.

Lord, You hear the prayers of Your people.
I will pray continually for those I love.

A SAFE PLACE

Trust in him at all times, you people; pour out your hearts to him, for God is our refuge.

PSALM 62:8

Where is the safe place in your home? Where do you run when the weatherman says it's time to take cover or the tornado alarms go off in your community? The answer is probably contingent on the type of home in which you live. You may move to a room without windows, to a bathroom, or to a lower level. Given enough time, you might have to leave your home completely and seek shelter elsewhere.

Whatever your particular living arrangements, you have most likely considered various scenarios and know the location of your safe place. This kind of knowledge can take a lot of the fear out of intense situations; knowing where to go can make all the difference.

Times of crisis are going to come into our lives. We may not all encounter the exact same scenario, but if we are in Christ, we all have the same safe place. We all have different backgrounds, different living situations, and different coping strategies, but God is a refuge for every one of us.

Have you suffered a terrible loss? God is your safe place. Have you been betrayed or abandoned? God is your safe place. Maybe you're struggling with life and just need a place to pour out your heart and be heard. God is your safe place.

Security is often listed as one of the greatest needs for women. This includes financial, physical, and emotional security. We were created with the need to feel safe, and God Himself meets that need. When it's time to take cover and the alarms are sounding, run to Him.

No one is capable of being my refuge, Lord. Nothing in this world can offer me security. You alone are my refuge in every situation. Thank You for being my safe place in an often scary world.

TAKE A MESSAGE

*The LORD said to me, "Write my answer plainly on tablets,
so that a runner can carry the correct message to others."*

HABAKKUK 2:2 NLT

How good are you at taking a message? Before folks could leave a voice mail or send a text, whoever answered the phone had to be able to write down all of the pertinent information and relay it accurately to the intended recipient. That's why every phone had a pen and paper beside it.

A poorly relayed message can cause problems. Sometimes you're given just enough information to completely misunderstand the message. You might remember that when you were sixteen, a message saying that "some guy called" was absolutely unacceptable. It turns out that details are important.

God used prophets to relay messages to His people. It goes without saying that when you're passing on a message from God Himself, you probably want to be accurate. God gave Habakkuk very specific directions; he was to write the message clearly so there would be no misunderstandings. The message was to be absolutely correct when the runner relayed it from Habakkuk to the people.

Likewise, we need to be careful relaying God's Word to others. Have you ever listened to a sermon or received advice from a friend that turned out to be out of line with the Word of God? Messing with the message is a dangerous thing. Revelation 22:18–19 lists the severe consequences for someone who takes away from or adds to God's Word. Let's be sure we are passing on only what God has said—nothing more and nothing less.

*I want to be careful, Lord, to pass on only what You have
plainly said. Do not let me confuse Your Word with my
own opinion. Let me relay only a message of truth.*

SLOW COOKING

Wait for the LORD; be strong and take heart and wait for the LORD.

PSALM 27:14

The slow cooker is somewhat of a mixed blessing. It makes dinner easy and virtually stress free, but it also makes your home smell delicious hours before the meal is actually ready to be eaten. Just try to put a roast with veggies and potatoes in the crock at 9:00 a.m. and see if your family isn't asking to eat it by noon. The problem is that the meal won't be edible until around 5:00 p.m. Unfortunately, everyone just has to wait.

Waiting when you're hungry and you know good things are coming isn't easy. It's tempting to just sit around and stare at the slow cooker. Oh, but how wonderful is that meal when you allow it to do what it needs to do in order for it to be completely ready? How hungry for it are you when it's finally placed before you? Aren't you always glad you waited?

Christ-followers know that something really good is coming. We catch glimpses now and then. The Bible says that God has "set eternity in the human heart" (Ecclesiastes 3:11). We long for the beauty that awaits us, and at times we think we want it all right now. It's not easy to wait.

Life can be difficult and relationships strained, and we just want Jesus to come back. New wounds are inflicted and old pains resurface. We get tired of the way people choose cruelty over kindness and grudges over grace. Forgiveness feels foreign, and we're ready for the suffering to end. We long for Him to swoop in and save the day because we're tired of the waiting.

Could it be that, in our waiting, we spend too much time staring at the skies, longing for our rescue when we should be busying ourselves making sure others are just as ready for His return? Could it be that His delay is actually an act of mercy? The fact is that God is restraining Himself because He doesn't want anyone to perish (2 Peter 3:9).

Each day that the Lord tarries is another twenty-four-hour period when someone else continues to have a chance to choose Him. Won't we be glad we waited?

It's not easy to wait for You, Lord, but I know Your timing is perfect. Give me the strength and faith to finish my race well.

LIVING IN COMMUNITY

Brothers and sisters, choose seven men from among you who are known to be
full of the Spirit and wisdom. We will turn this responsibility over to them.

ACTS 6:3

Do you ever find yourself intimidated by other women? Are you embarrassed when other moms show up to a playdate with coolers full of healthy snacks and bottles of water when all you brought was a ziplock bag full of cheese crackers and a desperate hope for a sanitary water fountain? You're not the only one; we all have our strong suits, and snack packing isn't everyone's. We just need friends who see our struggle and pack extra snacks for our kids; those women are a blessing.

In Acts 6, the church was growing quickly, and some things began to slip through the cracks. Due to a large number of people and a language barrier, the Greek-speaking Jews were upset that their widows were being neglected. They wanted the apostles to come in and fix the problem.

The solution the apostles came up with was for the people within that community to rise up and take on that responsibility for themselves. That is the beauty of a community. The people living within it know the needs of the people and, often, how to help.

You and I are a community. Some women are comfortable with the concept of community. They know the signs of a mama who's on the edge, because they've been there. They recognize the desperation in her eyes because they've seen it in the mirror. They're great at Mom's Night Out and small talk in the halls at school and church. They sip their coffee and smile as they sit on the bleachers at their children's sporting events. Yet, some women still struggle with living in community.

It should break our hearts that so many women are lonely. How many would like to be a part of a community where other ladies were navigating similar circumstances? It just takes one person stepping out of her comfort zone and saying, "You're not alone." Let's rise up and help our sisters doing life right alongside us.

You didn't create us to do life alone, Lord. Help me to live in community with those around me.

CRUMPLE BURGERS

The heart of man plans his way, but the LORD establishes his steps.

PROVERBS 16:9 ESV

We've all heard the saying "When life gives you lemons, make lemonade." If you're not a lemonade drinker, here's another version for you: "When you planned to make sloppy joes, you've already browned your beef, but you forgot the sauce, make crumple burgers." Okay, it's not very catchy, but the sentiment is the same. You've surely had a dinnertime experience similar to this one:

You're preparing sloppy joes for dinner. At the last moment you realize you failed to purchase the needed sauce for the dish. Your family is hungry and has expectations of a certain meal being placed on the table. What do you do? You pile that ground beef on a hamburger bun, call it a "crumple burger," and lead your family in giving thanks. And you hide your surprise and delight when the spouse and kids love it!

We can do all the planning and prep work we want, but sometimes it just doesn't happen the way we thought it would. We've all been frustrated or disappointed by something that didn't turn out how we had hoped. It can be difficult to accept that we may not end up with the relationship we desired, the job we applied for, or the life we had imagined. Through the prophet Isaiah, God told us that His ways are higher than anything we can imagine (Isaiah 55:8), and through the prophet Jeremiah we learn that His plans are good (Jeremiah 29:11).

As we go about our lives making plans, let's be open to God's intervention. No matter how great our dreams or visions may seem, we know that God can do so much more than anything we could imagine (Ephesians 3:20). When life doesn't meet our expectations, let's be open to the idea that God is at work. What He has planned may seem like a plan B dinner to us, but it will be a part of His perfect plan A, and it will be good.

*I'm tempted to panic when things don't go the way
I think they should, Lord. Teach me to trust You
more. Your plan for my life is the plan I want.*

POWER LINES

They are not connected to Christ, the head of the body. For he holds the whole body together with its joints and ligaments, and it grows as God nourishes it.

COLOSSIANS 2:19 NLT

How do you feel when your electricity goes out? When a storm is raging, and suddenly a power line is down and you're in the dark? Something amazing could be happening in the world and you wouldn't even know! What about when the Wi-Fi isn't working properly? It's a weird feeling being disconnected from the outside world, isn't it? Some of us have palpitations if our Internet goes down for even an hour and we're forced to go to sleep without our final Facebook check. What if someone posts a picture of their bedtime snack and we miss it?

The same is true for families. It's always a hard transition when a child goes to college, someone gets married, or a friend moves for a job. Suddenly, those connections don't seem as secure, and it can be a little scary. We might feel like things are falling apart as people begin spreading their wings and going their own ways. We long to feel connected to other people.

The body of Christ is made up of a variety of people. We look and think differently; we have different gifts. We might feel, at times, as if we're not connected at all. That can be quite unsettling. The good news is that no believer is ever left to fend for him- or herself. No one is ever left in the dark. As a family of believers, we are all connected to Christ and, through Him, to each other. He is the power source for each of us.

Christ holds us together, and He nourishes us so that we continue to grow closer to one another. Paul told the Colossians that "in [Christ] all things hold together" (Colossians 1:17). We don't have to worry about being alone or separated from Him. We're always connected to the power source.

*No matter what storms come, Lord, Your power will
never fail and You will never leave me stranded in
the dark. Thank You for holding us all together.*

FOLLOW THE RECIPE

*Your ears shall hear a word behind you, saying, "This is the way, walk
in it," when you turn to the right or when you turn to the left.*

ISAIAH 30:21 ESV

Perhaps during your college years, cooking was by trial and error. You may have had a general idea of the ingredients but had to experiment with the amounts. You probably ate several mediocre dishes before discovering the perfect combination of flavors. Then something wonderful took place: you bought your first cookbook so you could make whatever you wanted by simply following the recipe. Now you don't have to reinvent the wheel; you just do what the recipe tells you to do.

It's not God's desire to hide His will from us. We don't have to try random things in an attempt to figure it out. We don't have to walk down various paths and hope that we eventually end up in the right place. The prophet Isaiah told God's people that He would hear them when they called to Him and that He would not hide Himself (Isaiah 30:19-20). Not only would He not hide Himself, but He would be with them step by step, and He would help them stay on the right path.

Wouldn't that be wonderful? You start to stray off the straight and narrow and you hear a voice saying, *Not that way.* Perhaps you have a difficult choice to make. You're leaning toward one option and you hear a voice advising, *Yes, that's the way.* What if you didn't have to question everything all the time and you could just do what the voice told you to do? The good news is that's how you were meant to live.

We don't have to live by trial and error. God has not hidden Himself from us. He has made His will known through His Word, and we have His guidance through the Holy Spirit. If we'll only read our Bibles and pray continually, we will hear His voice behind us saying, *This is the way; walk in it.*

I always end up lost when I try to make it on my own, Lord.
Speak to me, guide me, and keep me on Your way.

THE SNACK DRAWER

When we get together, I want to encourage you in your faith,
but I also want to be encouraged by yours.

ROMANS 1:12 NLT

When you gather as a family for a substantial meal, chances are you'll have access to enough food to keep you satisfied for quite some time. Bacon and eggs for breakfast or a baked potato and salad for lunch. Dinner may include a hearty main course, some side dishes, and a dessert. The food replenishes our bodies, and the fellowship revitalizes our spirits.

These meals are blessings, but on most days, when the meals are lighter, we begin searching the refrigerator or pantry for a snack at various times during the day. We don't need to sit down with a bunch of people and partake of a feast; we just need a little something to get us through the moment.

Some families make it easy by having a snack drawer. When someone's stomach is feeling a little empty or they just need something to help them make it to the next meal, they can grab a granola bar or a pack of crackers. It's nice to have something when your energy is low.

Christians are instructed to not neglect gathering together with other believers (Hebrews 10:25). Most of us understand the importance of this and make it a habit to meet regularly with our local church body. We are able to replenish our spirits through fellowship, and if we're lucky, a potluck will be involved.

While these times of corporate worship are vital to our faith and are acts of obedience to Scripture, there will be times when we need something in between these scheduled meetings. We need godly friends we can turn to when life is hard. We need people close to us with wisdom we can draw from, and we need to be a source of encouragement and wisdom to others.

Godly friends are vital in a believer's life. Let's seek them out and seek to be them.

Thank You, Lord, for the gift of godly friends who sustain me during difficult seasons. I pray that I can be a source of encouragement to others.

LEGOS ON THE FLOOR

Put on the whole armor of God, that you may be able to stand against the schemes of the devil.

EPHESIANS 6:11 ESV

Seasoned mothers know that you never enter a child's bedroom without proper footwear. If you've ever forgotten this hard-and-fast rule, you may have had the unfortunate experience of stepping on a Lego as you attempted to sneak out of the bedroom of a sleeping child. It usually goes something like this: you've just spent forty-five minutes reading, singing, or patting your child on the back. He finally falls asleep, and you begin the most dangerous part of the process: exiting the room. You hold your breath as you slowly move toward the door; your heart is beating wildly. Freedom is in sight. You're almost there!

Then you step on the dreaded Lego lying on the floor. You fall to the ground and writhe in silent anguish, knowing that the slightest noise will awaken your child, and it will all be for naught. You drag your wounded body out of the room, close the door, and lie in the hallway, certain that the Lego is permanently embedded in your foot. Never again will you enter such dangerous territory without protection.

We have an Enemy who is constantly setting traps and hoping we will step into them. He is counting on us walking around unprotected. He will leave things in our paths to harm us, take things from us, distract us, and tempt us. Paul warned believers about these snares of the devil (2 Timothy 2:26).

God has given us everything we need to avoid the pain of these pitfalls. Paul described all the ways we can protect ourselves: truth, righteousness, faith, salvation, and the sword of the Spirit are all tools at our disposal. We are to use these tools to navigate dangerous territory; we would be foolish to attempt to make it through unprotected.

We don't have to tiptoe our way through this world hoping we don't step on a land mine hidden like a Lego in the carpet. We can walk boldly, knowing that we have put on the proper protection.

Lord, keep me in Your Word and in Your will so I'm properly protected from the Enemy's hidden snares.

TEND YOUR OWN GARDEN

But as for you, continue in what you have learned and have
firmly believed, knowing from whom you learned it.

2 TIMOTHY 3:14 ESV

Aunt Karen didn't put up with any gossiping around her. If anyone started talking about someone else's business, she was quick to interrupt and say, "Hope you're tending your own garden as much as you're tending their garden." In other words, everyone needed to mind their own business.

In 2 Timothy, Paul warned believers about some evils to come. He spoke of deceivers and swindlers, gossips and abusers, those who were conceited and reckless. With every word, we can probably name a person with that trait.

Lack of self-control? *You know, that describes so-and-so, and she probably doesn't know it, so I should call her out. Preach it, Paul.* We read a passage like that, and our focus quickly goes to others. But Paul set his readers straight: he told us what other folks were doing, and then he said, "But as for you . . ." Suddenly, the focus is right back on us, and we squirm in our seat just a little.

Whatever craziness is swirling around, whatever foolishness is being shared, whatever fear is spreading like wildfire, or whatever other people are choosing to do, say, or think—"Continue in what you have learned and firmly believed."

During those days when the gossip is flowing and the anger is rising, take a deep breath. When folks begin to panic and the news is downright scary, just remember. When tongues are wagging, fingers are pointing, and you're feeling under attack . . .

As for you . . .

Teach me, Lord, to tend my own garden. Forgive me for the times when I
have been quick to find fault in others instead of checking my own heart.

LEFTOVERS

But they did not listen to Moses. Some left part of it till the morning,
and it bred worms and stank. And Moses was angry with them.

Exodus 16:20 esv

Have you ever brought home leftovers from your favorite restaurant, put them in your refrigerator, and then forgot about them? You had every intention of eating them, but you never got around to it. Maybe you thought they would stay fresh longer than they did, or perhaps you're just really bad about cleaning out your fridge.

A friend once came to my house to watch my child while I went to a doctor's appointment. The visit went longer than expected, and the friend was at my house during lunch time. Before driving home, I texted to apologize, and she replied, "No problem. I just helped myself to some of your leftover meatloaf." For the life of me, I couldn't remember the last time I had made meatloaf. Then I realized I had a problem.

The children of Israel have the ultimate story of leftovers gone bad. God provided for them by having manna appear each morning. They were to go out each day and gather enough for that day's consumption, no more and no less. Seems easy enough, right? The Israelites disobeyed and left some of it until morning.

It could be that they were greedy and gathered more than they could eat in a day's time. Maybe they worried that God would not provide more the next day and, therefore, attempted to save some. Whether greed or doubt caused them to leave the manna to rot, the end result was the same. They sinned against God by disobeying His instructions on how to handle the manna.

We won't always understand the reasoning behind some of God's commands, but our obedience should never be based on our understanding. Let's obey right away, all the way, and with a good attitude, knowing that the consequences of disobedience stink!

*I don't need to know the how and the why of every command
You give, Lord. I will obey You even when I don't understand.*

HOUSE SITTING

Please deliver me from the hand of my brother, from the hand of Esau, for I
fear him, that he may come and attack me, the mothers with the children.

GENESIS 32:11 ESV

What do you fear? Heights, tight spaces, or clowns? Maybe public speaking, mice, or airplanes distress you. We all have something that scares us. Once, while housesitting for me, my father sent me a picture of a snake that had slithered out from behind the garage. The photo came to my phone along with the caption, "Don't worry. I've already put the For Sale sign in the yard." Fear can be a powerful thing. What do we do when we encounter fear?

Adam was afraid in Genesis 3, and he hid in the bushes. Sarah was afraid in Genesis 18, and she lied. Lot was afraid in Genesis 19, and he hid in a cave. Isaac was afraid in Genesis 26, and he lied. That seems to be the go-to response to fear. We hide or we lie, and sometimes we do both. What else are we supposed to do?

How exactly should we respond when fear rears its ugly head, when we get that diagnosis, or when there is more month than money? How do we act when friends move away, jobs are eliminated, or our hearts are broken?

We could lie and say that everything is fine. We can convince ourselves and others that we can handle it on our own. We could always hide, stay in our pajamas and binge-watch the latest release on Netflix. We can skip church, cancel plans with friends, and gorge ourselves on chips and salsa. The truth is that the Enemy would love for us to lie and hide. The problem with that is that lying and hiding never take away the fear; they only serve to cover it in shame. So what should we do when we feel the anxiety creep in and the tension take over?

We could, like Jacob, immediately turn to God (Genesis 32:9). We could make prayer our first response. Then we could acknowledge our place before God and confess our fears to Him (Genesis 32:10–11). What would happen if we stopped playing the I'm-okay-you're-okay game and were open with our fears? Finally, we need to remember God's promises (Genesis 32:12).

Let's begin living boldly and unafraid.

Fear, left unchecked, can invade and take over. When fear tries to have its way with me, Lord, I will remind myself of Your promises.

UTENSIL

INSIDE SCOOP

"How can I," he said, "unless someone explains it to me?"
So he invited Philip to come up and sit with him.

There are certain things you just can't know unless someone tells you. As the saying goes, "You don't know what you don't know." With that in mind, here are some ways to up your breakfast game: Any egg dish needs hot sauce. Use cinnamon bread when making French toast. Sprinkle sugar in your grits before serving. Sausage biscuits must have grape jelly. And always butter your chocolate toaster pastries.

Sometimes people just assume that everyone is privy to the same information. Or perhaps they think they must have certain training or education to share with others. That's just not the case. It's our responsibility to share what we know with those around us. God will give us opportunities to share. In the book of Acts, the Lord sent Philip to an Ethiopian official. As Philip approached, he could hear the official reading the book of Isaiah.

The Lord knew that the man needed someone to come alongside him and help make sense of it all. Philip asked if the man understood what he was reading, and he responded, "How can I unless someone explains it to me?" The Ethiopian then invited Philip to sit with him, giving Philip the opportunity to tell the man about Jesus.

Think about the people you interact with on a daily basis. Who in your circle of influence needs you to share with them? Family members, friends, coworkers, the cashier at the grocery store? Could it be that God placed you in their path so you could tell them about Jesus? Take the time to sit with them. Share what you know. Share *who* you know. How else will they understand?

Ask God for opportunities to share Jesus with others. Then pray for the boldness to embrace those opportunities. And while you're at it, make sure they know to butter their chocolate Pop-Tarts.

You don't need me to bring others to You, Lord,
but You choose to use me anyway. Thank You for
the privilege of being a part of Your work.

THE TELEPHONE GAME

*Now these Jews were more noble than those in Thessalonica; they received the word
with all eagerness, examining the Scriptures daily to see if these things were so.*

ACTS 17:11 ESV

The Telephone Game is often played at sleepovers and church lock-ins. One person thinks up a random phrase or sentence and whispers it into the ear of the next person. That person whispers what they believe the first person said into the ear of the next person. This is repeated around a circle of people until the final person states out loud what they believe to be the original phrase or statement. As you can imagine, the quotation often gets slightly distorted each time it's repeated. The final one to hear the message compares his or her version with that of the person who created the original message.

There are different reasons why a message may be altered from one person to another. Maybe the one hearing the message simply misunderstands. Perhaps the one relaying the message doesn't speak clearly or misunderstands the message himself. Sadly, some people will purposely give a wrong message to mislead people. This reminds us of the wolves in sheep's clothing Jesus warned us about (Matthew 7:15).

There are messages that we want to be certain we understand correctly. When someone speaks concerning the things of God, we need to go straight to God's Word to see if what we're hearing is true to what God has said. Scripture cuts to the truth like a "double-edged sword" (Hebrews 4:12). This means that if someone says something or if we ourselves read something that seems contradictory, we should immediately examine God's Word further and seek clarification.

We are blessed to have knowledgeable preachers and teachers. We can choose from a plethora of studies to do and conferences to attend. None of these probably compared to hearing the apostle Paul talk about Jesus, yet even he commended the

Bereans and called them noble because of their diligence in comparing what they heard him say to what God said. This practice would be beneficial for us as well.

Thank You, Lord, for those who have been gifted with the ability to teach and preach. Remind me to always use wisdom and discernment as I compare what I hear with what You have said in Your Word.

DIRTY LAUNDRY

Pray without ceasing.

1 Thessalonians 5:17 esv

Laundry is one of those never-ending tasks. It seems to multiply in the hamper when nobody's watching. Just when you think the job is done, you find more behind a closet door or under a bed. Or you really do finish it, but then everyone changes into their pajamas. Before you even fall asleep, half a load is already waiting for you to do the next day. Any time a parent goes missing, someone should check the laundry room because he or she has probably been buried alive.

Let's face it: doing laundry continually is the only way to keep it under control. If you have ever taken a laundry break, then you know it can become overwhelming in a hurry. It's also important to do it completely. We all know what happens if we leave wet items in the washing machine—it isn't pretty. That load of towels doesn't need one more spin in the dryer; that's just an easy way to delay folding them. We all try the same tricks, don't we?

Prayer works much the same way. It was never meant to be a one-and-done scenario. Prayer is an ongoing form of communication between our Father and us. Problems multiply faster than dirty towels in the bathroom hamper when we don't deal with them prayerfully. We weren't meant to bear our burdens alone, and we feel overwhelmed in a hurry when we try. Paul knew what he was talking about when he instructed us to pray continually.

Let's not limit prayer to Sunday mornings and scary moments. Let's live in a continual state of prayer. Then when some unexpected need arises, our response can be, *Lord, since we're talking anyway, I need to tell You about this.* Pray without ceasing, and while you're at it, throw a load of laundry in the machine.

I come confidently to You, Lord, knowing You hear my prayers and that You will answer when I call. I can pray without ceasing, knowing that You're always listening.

NOTHING TO EAT

The people spoke against God and against Moses, "Why have you
brought us up out of Egypt to die in the wilderness? For there is no
food and no water, and we loathe this worthless food."

NUMBERS 21:5 ESV

Have you ever had a hankering for something to eat only to rummage through the kitchen and declare that "there wasn't anything"? There were leftovers from dinner, some fruit in a bowl, and chips in the pantry. The problem is that you'd already had those things, and they no longer excited you; so you concluded that there was nothing to eat.

That's what we do, isn't it? Something excites us for a while, and then we grow bored with it. What enthralled us at one point becomes a nuisance later. We get so accustomed to the way things are that we fail to see the blessings. We feel entitled to *more*. We begin to have a distorted view of our current situation and an ungratefulness regarding the things God has done.

The worthless food that the people were complaining about was the bread God rained down from heaven. Scripture says that it tasted like wafers made with honey (Exodus 16:31). It was the blessing God provided even while the Israelites were longing for the days when they were in Egypt, where they sat and ate meat until they were full (Exodus 16:3). The problem was that they were slaves in Egypt and were not recalling the situation accurately at all!

Why do we treasure the things of the world and remember them as more than they were, while at the same time trivializing the things of God and making them less than they were? It's because Satan is a deceiver who seeks to plant seeds of doubt and ungratefulness in the hearts of God's people.

Let's ask God to open our eyes to the blessings around us. We need to stop romanticizing the past and see that God is doing great things at this very moment. Let's not miss them!

I don't want to take Your blessings for granted, Lord. Every good and perfect gift comes from You. Help me to stop looking back and to look for the blessings You're giving to me today.

MANY HANDS

Two are better than one, because they have a good reward for
their toil. For if they fall, one will lift up his fellow.

ECCLESIASTES 4:9–10 ESV

Have you ever walked into the kitchen after hosting a party or holiday meal and been overwhelmed by the mess before you? Cleaning the kitchen can be a daunting task. You think you've cleaned up all the dishes, but there are more on the table. You need to put away leftovers, but none of your plastic containers seem to have lids. There is work to be done everywhere you look. It's a seemingly impossible task, and one person should not do it alone.

How much easier is the work when other people help? One person can tackle the trash while another gathers dirty dishes. Someone can put away leftovers while another person sweeps the floor. The work is done much faster with help. After all, as the saying goes, many hands make light work. Just another person's presence can make a job seem doable!

If you were to look around you at all the needs in your family, church, and community, you would feel completely overwhelmed. One person can't possibly minister to every hurt, provide for every financial need, and share the gospel with every lost soul. There is ministry to be done everywhere you look, and God never intended for it to be a one-person job.

The body of Christ is made up of many people with different skill sets and varying personalities who are in different seasons of life. None of us can do the job on our own. But when we work together, we can have a good reward for our efforts. You can minister to someone with whom I could not. I can connect with a person with whom someone else may not.

We don't have to be heroes rushing in to save the day for everyone. We just need to do our part; I do what I'm called to do and you do what God instructs you to do. Together we can do the Lord's work until He comes.

Not everyone can be the star of the show, Lord. Teach me to be a team player. Show me the part I need to play in Your perfect plan, and give me what I need to do it well.

WHEN LIFE IS LOUD

Be silent before the Sovereign Lord.

ZEPHANIAH 1:7

Does your life ever seem incredibly loud? Maybe you're surrounded by actual noises: people talking, dishwasher humming, and the television blaring. Or perhaps the noise is inside your head: anxiety, stress, guilt, and shame. Sometimes life can seem so loud that it drowns out the voice of God. We convince ourselves that we would be able to hear from Him if only other people were quieter or if the stresses of life would cease for just a moment. We think He could speak to us better if the neighbors would turn down the music or the kids would just take a nap.

Maybe you've endured one of those days when one child is watching cartoons with the volume on high while another is reading aloud, the cable guy is drilling a hole in the wall, and a potty-training toddler is making a puddle on the floor while simultaneously demanding a treat. Life is loud. No wonder we sometimes suspect that God is speaking but we just can't hear Him.

There is good news for those covered in noise. God never said to silence the sounds around us. He never instructed us to get our mess tidied up before we attempt to converse with Him. It isn't our world that needs to be silent; it's us. Everything doesn't need to suddenly be still in order for us to hear God; we are the ones who need to be still. We can do that because we have control over ourselves.

Maybe that speaks to you too. Does your life seem so loud that it drowns out the voice of the Father? It's safe to say that God can speak above whatever noise we have going on at the moment.

Speak to me above the noise of my life, Lord. When life is loud, I will quiet my heart so that I can hear what You would say to me.

GUACAMOLE

He is before all things, and in him all things hold together.

COLOSSIANS 1:17

Guacamole is one of those foods that people tend to either love or hate. Even those who relish the stuff would agree that several of the ingredients are on many people's "no, thank you" list: garlic, raw onion, avocado, and lemon juice. If a salad bar offered these ingredients individually, many diners would leave them untouched, but mix them together and the magic happens.

There's something about avocado that allows other ingredients with strong flavors to hold together in a way that makes sense and tastes great. All the ingredients create something together that they could never be individually.

It's tempting to look at people and judge whether or not they would mesh with us. Maybe they have a strong personality or they listen to a different kind of music. Perhaps we fear their structured way of doing things would never work with our free-spirited ways. It could be that we fall in love but are afraid to marry someone who seems to be our polar opposite. If it was all left up to us, many relationships would simply never work.

But when we let Jesus into our relationships, He can show us how we all fit together. He can enable us to see the beauty and gifts in each other and how important it is to have variety. If we let Him, Jesus can put us with people who will grow us in ways we never thought possible. We can be more beautiful together than we would ever be individually. Jesus can give us friendships and relationships that are as wonderful of a surprise as guacamole on a chip.

I miss out on beautiful relationships when I try to pick friends based on appearances. Surround me with the people You want in my life, Lord, and surprise me with the variety.

SPREADING THE NEWS

It gave me great joy when some believers came and testified about your
faithfulness to the truth, telling how you continue to walk in it.

3 JOHN v. 3

What types of stories are your favorite? Do you love a good scare, or are you a sucker for a romance? Maybe you love to laugh. Some people want to hear stories of believers walking in the truth. They want to hear word of people being faithful to what they believe and tales of folks coming to know the Christ they adore. Yes, if you want to fill certain individuals with joy, just sit with them and testify about saints being faithful to God.

There is something awe inspiring about hearing of someone in another country having a dream about Christ and believing. Stories of little children feeling the love of God and experiencing hope for the first time are simply the best. Then there are the stories of those who have been Christ-followers for some time and remained faithful in the face of tragedy. Many people have stood firm in the face of persecution. Who doesn't love a story that builds up the body of Christ and brings some joy to the hearts of the hearers?

The apostle John loved a good story as well, especially when it was about the faithfulness of his friend, Gaius. John experienced "great joy" when a group of believers came to give him word regarding Gaius. The believers were able to testify about his faithfulness to Christ and to what he had been taught.

All too often we are tempted to share the negative stories. The old newspaper adage, "If it bleeds, it leads," is a sad commentary on what keeps the attention of people. Let's not give in to the pressure to spread gloom and doom. Let our next story be one that brings the hearer joy by testifying to someone's faithfulness to God.

People everywhere are walking in truth and in faithfulness to You. Help me share those stories and spread some joy to Your people.

DAD'S VOICE

"My sheep hear my voice, and I know them, and they follow me."

JOHN 10:27 ESV

A dad's voice is instantly recognizable. You know your father when he calls you on the phone, and you could recognize his laugh in a crowd. When that voice yells your name, you drop everything to see what he needs because you don't ignore Dad's voice. He leaves you a voice mail saying, "It's Dad—call me," and you laugh because, of course it's Dad. Then, when he's gone, you play the last phone message over and over because there's something special about that man's voice.

A shepherd's voice is to his sheep like our dads' voices are to us. Multiple flocks of sheep can be kept in the same pasture, but when a shepherd opens the gate and calls, only that shepherd's sheep will come to him. The others will instantly know that it is not their shepherd, and they'll run away. This is the picture Jesus was painting when He said, "I know my sheep and my sheep know me" (John 10:14).

There are two aspects to recognizing a voice. One person must speak often, and the other person must be listening well. If you don't have a long history of your dad speaking to you, or if you chose to not listen, then his voice may not be instantly recognizable. If the shepherd doesn't make a habit of talking to the sheep, they will not learn his voice.

Jesus is constantly speaking to His children. They only reason we'd fail to know His voice is if we've made no attempt to listen. Let's be quick to listen when He speaks. We need to be able to distinguish His voice from other voices in the world. Others will try to lead us astray. They will come to the sheepfold, open the gate, and call our name. We need to know when it isn't our Shepherd so we can run the other way.

Lord, make Your voice stand out among
the many that seek to lead me astray.

THE SECRET INGREDIENT

I have been crucified with Christ and I no longer live, but Christ lives in me.

GALATIANS 2:20

Have you ever had a dish at a friend's house or a restaurant that had a certain flavor you couldn't quite name? Maybe you asked what it was and were told that there was a secret ingredient. You wanted to replicate it at home but had the hardest time because of that one unknown addition. It can be frustrating being served a dish that you can't seem to replicate.

Have you ever met a person and wondered how they were able to keep a positive attitude? Carry on after an unthinkable tragedy? Forgive a betrayal? Overcome a difficult past? We've all watched someone walk through a season of suffering and wondered how they did it. There must be a secret ingredient, right?

There *is* a secret ingredient for navigating life in a broken world, and the secret is Christ. The world would have us believe that it's money, beauty, or fame, but those things will never produce the result we long for in our lives. The answer has always been and will always be Christ.

Unlike a chef at a fancy restaurant, we should want others to know the secret. When someone asks how we are able to put one foot in front of the other, we should be quick to name Christ. We can't credit our own strength or willpower. We're not just pulling ourselves up by the bootstraps. The secret to life is Christ dwelling in us. When it comes to finding purpose and direction in life, we want others to know the recipe. What is the answer to forgiving the unforgivable? Christ in you. How does a person begin again when everything has been stripped away? Christ living in them. Whatever someone is trying to figure out, Christ is the answer. He is always the secret ingredient.

You're the answer to every issue we face, Lord. You're the only source of purpose and peace. You are the secret ingredient to everything we seek in this life.

RUBBER BOOTS

Build houses and live in them; plant gardens and eat their produce.

Let's say that you had big plans to run errands, go shopping, or go out with friends on a particular day. How would you feel if you woke up on the morning of that day to find that it was pouring down rain? You could cancel the plans and stay inside where it was safe and warm. You might reschedule your plans for a day with more pleasant weather.

Or you could put on your rubber boots and head on out into the rain! Once you give yourself permission to get your feet wet, you feel so much better about being out in the world. Realizing that it's okay to get a little messy is freeing.

We can easily get images in our head of how we think our lives will look. We begin making plans at an early age for our careers, our families, and the mark we will make on the world. We make decisions and begin working in a certain direction. What if it doesn't work out like it was supposed to in our carefully laid plans?

How do we respond when life rains on our parade? Do we throw in the towel, cancel our plans, and hide ourselves away from the world? Do we postpone our dreams for a better day or an easier time? It's tempting, isn't it?

When the people of Israel were carried captive into a foreign land, all their plans for their lives seemed to be for naught. How were they to carry on when their lives looked so different from how they thought they would look?

God told His people to keep on keepin' on! He told them to build lives in the communities where they found themselves: Build houses and live in them. Plant gardens and enjoy the produce. Marry and have children.

Sometimes we end up in places we never thought we would find ourselves. It may be a physical location, a broken relationship, or an unfulfilling career. We can hide away and just pass the time until our "real lives" begin. Or we can embrace where God has us at the moment.

We can build homes, help those in need, and seek to make disciples. We can do the work of God wherever we are, and if it rains, we put on our rain boots.

*Life doesn't always turn out the way I plan, Lord. Give
me the strength I need to embrace Your plan for me.*

BAKED CUSTARD

It is not good for a person to be without knowledge, and he who hurries his footsteps errs.

PROVERBS 19:2 NASB

Egg custard pudding is one of the easiest things to make. It involves eggs, milk, sugar, and vanilla all mixed together with a sprinkling of nutmeg on top. With a little guidance, anyone can make it. The step-by-step instructions may not be complicated, but you need to know something if you're going to make it: it takes a sweet forever in the oven, and then more time on top of that to cool down.

To get the proper creamy texture that you desire, the custard needs to bake "low and slow." Depending on your oven, it can take up to an hour and a half. Then you must remove it from the oven, place it on a cooling rack, and allow it to cool completely. It's a slow process, and there's no way around it. If you're tempted to raise the oven temperature and cook it faster, be warned that it doesn't work. Do you think maybe you'll make a double batch and cook two at a time? Sorry, that effort will fail too.

Some things in life can't be rushed, and we're likely to make mistakes when we try. Scripture warns believers that we'll err when we hurry. We can't rush into relationships with people without getting to know them. We shouldn't throw ourselves into a situation without taking the time to understand it.

In an example about building a tower, Jesus asked, "Won't you first sit down and estimate the cost?" (Luke 14:28). It's important to take stock of a situation and make a plan. Otherwise, we risk making foolish mistakes and not benefiting anyone. Fast and furious may seem more exciting, but low and slow is the way to go.

We live in a world where being first or being the fastest is often praised. Slow me down, Lord! Don't let me rush in unprepared; teach me to count the cost.

HIDE-AND-SEEK

If you look for me wholeheartedly, you will find me.

JEREMIAH 29:13 NLT

We spend so much of our lives hiding things. Have you ever purchased a Christmas gift for someone and hidden it so well that you completely forgot about it until you came across it again in March? As a teenager, did you know how to hide a diary in places where no one would ever discover it? Even now, as an adult, do you know exactly where to hide in order to eat your candy bar in secret? It's okay; we've all done it.

We have all placed an item somewhere for safekeeping so we could easily retrieve it when needed only to completely forget where we put it. Whether it's something you've hidden or someone else has hidden, trying to find hidden things can be annoying.

While things are often hidden from us, there are also times when we look for things that are in plain sight. It's like playing hide-and-seek with a toddler. You could sit in a recliner in plain view and cover yourself with a blanket, but the toddler will look behind tables, in bathtubs, and under rugs. Meanwhile, you haven't moved since the last time the child saw you. Let's just say the game lasts way longer than it probably should.

Have you ever found yourself on a dark day wondering where God went? He can be hard to see in the midst of trials and pain. Suffering can cloud our vision until we're looking for God everywhere except where He is—right in front of us. God promises that He'll never leave us (Deuteronomy 31:6). We can know that God is right where He has always been.

God is still present no matter what a day may bring. God does not hide Himself from us. He can be found by anyone whose heart seeks Him.

I'm so glad You don't play games, Lord. Thank You for
allowing Yourself to be found by all who seek You.

GRANNY AND GRANDDADDY

Do not forget to show hospitality to strangers, for by so doing some
people have shown hospitality to angels without knowing it.

HEBREWS 13:2

Perhaps your childhood included this cozy scene: Granny has the fridge stocked with your favorite beverage, and there are chocolate chip cookies fresh from the oven. You feel perfectly comfortable sleeping in late, walking around in your pajamas, and sitting at the kitchen table watching Granddaddy make homemade biscuits.

As an adult, Granny and Granddaddy's house is just as comfortable. You can put your feet on the furniture, help yourself to the pantry, and enjoy a lazy day together. There's something about a place where the coffee is always fresh and the conversation is always candid that makes a person want to keep coming back for more. Hospitality is irresistible.

Hospitality is important to God, and it should extend to more than just family members. Friends, acquaintances, and even complete strangers should be beneficiaries as well. When is the last time you invited someone new to sit at your dinner table? Why not invite someone who needs a break to come visit and be pampered?

Some people's lives are difficult every hour of every day, and they would benefit greatly from some good old-fashioned hospitality. A meal made and served with love, some good food and laughter, and someone else to clean up the kitchen can serve as a balm to a weary soul. Hospitality doesn't have to be limited to within the walls of our home. A batch of cookies delivered to a new neighbor or a sack lunch to the stranger standing on the street corner also constitutes hospitality. We never know when it may be an angel enjoying one of our famous chicken salad sandwiches.

We live in a world that teaches us to fear strangers, Lord.
Show me ways I can show them hospitality instead.

FIRST AID

"It was I who taught Ephraim to walk, taking them by the arms;
but they did not realize it was I who healed them."

HOSEA 11:3

If you have any children in your life, you're aware of their obsession with Band-Aids. Many little people cheer the opening of a new box featuring television characters, princes and princesses, or action figures. Some children may insist on putting a bandage on even the smallest of injury and wearing it as a badge of honor long after the tiny wound has healed.

In the same way, God's people continued to act wounded long after God had healed them. Hosea 11 shows that God became frustrated that His people did not seem to grasp how He cared for them. The Lord called them, but they continued to walk away. They chose idols even though it was God who had taught them to walk. God had healed their wounds, but they didn't seem to know it.

The word *healed* here includes a restored favor with God as well as the healing of individual infirmities. When God heals someone, that person is healed completely. The Israelites continued to walk under the burden of sin and shame; all the while, God had already redeemed and restored them. Can you relate?

How many people are walking around feeling broken, not knowing that God has already healed them? How many live with Satan whispering guilt in their ears over past mistakes, not realizing that they have been restored? We have an Enemy who wants us to feel broken beyond repair. He doesn't want us to grasp the magnitude of healing and how it would change the way we go about our lives.

Our God is a God of grace. If you are a Christ-follower, you need to know that you have been healed. His blood has made you healthy, whole, and restored. Don't let the Enemy make you believe otherwise. The Lord has healed you.

Thank You, Lord, for the healing power of Your love.
You mend the broken and strengthen the weak.
May I walk in the freedom of that healing.

BITE-SIZE PIECES

Beginning with Moses and all the Prophets, he explained to them
what was said in all the Scriptures concerning himself.

LUKE 24:27

Choking hazards are a big deal when you're feeding small children, and no one can blame a young mother for being a bit neurotic when it comes to cutting food into bite-size pieces. Maybe you can relate: you rarely catch up on laundry and you can never find a sippy cup when you need one, but you're obsessed with cutting every hot dog, grape, or carrot into noncircular, appropriately sized chunks. You realize that breaking things down makes them easier to swallow.

We might feel a little intimidated when we first approach the Word of God. There are parables, people, and poems. Perhaps there are names we can't pronounce or places we don't recognize. When we view it as a whole, the Bible may seem like too much. The key is to take it in a little at a time.

The men Jesus encountered on the road to Emmaus were confused over the things that had taken place. They were familiar with Scripture and had listened to Jesus' teachings, but they could not understand what had just happened. It all must have been incredibly overwhelming.

Jesus did not tell them to go back and reread the Scriptures, review their notes from His sermons, or spend more time in the temple. The Bible tells us that He began with Moses and broke down each passage of Scripture concerning Himself so they could digest what had happened and what would soon take place. To make it go down even easier, He opened their minds so that they could understand (Luke 24:45).

We could read our Bibles from cover to cover time and time again and still not fully take in everything written in those pages. The Word is a never-ending course of study. We can ask God to open our minds, break it into bite-size chunks, and explain it to us one piece at a time.

I long to understand Your Word, Lord. Give me the wisdom and discernment I need. Open my mind so I can know You more.

BEING PREPARED

*In your hearts revere Christ as Lord. Always be prepared to give an answer to everyone who
asks you to give the reason for the hope that you have. But do this with gentleness and respect.*

1 PETER 3:15

How would you rate your skills in terms of preparedness? Are you the type who
will run to the store to buy bread and milk at the threat of snow? On an outing
with the family, do you pack enough supplies to survive in the wilderness for ten days?
If a friend were ill, could you make them a meal complete with dessert from the items
in your well-stocked pantry?

Certain individuals have the gift of preparedness. They may stockpile enough food
to live completely off the grid if necessary. They probably have everything they need to
ride out an unexpected snowstorm. It's always nice to live close to one of these people.
To be honest, unless it is revealed that coffee and chocolate really are the secret to sus-
taining life, I'm pretty much in trouble.

God may not tell us to fill our root cellars with vegetables in case of an emergency,
but He does instruct us to always be prepared. We are to always be ready, in every
situation and interaction, to tell people about the hope we have in Christ. We never
know when someone desperate for some hope will cross our path and look to us for an
answer. Scripture doesn't tell us to be prepared with the e-mail address of someone they
can contact. It doesn't advise us to pass along the name and number of the local church.
The Bible does not command us to suggest a good book or some inspirational movie.
Yes, referrals are appropriate in some cases; still, we are all called to be prepared with
"an answer" for the hope we have in Christ.

What will we say when someone asks us about our faith? Will they know where to go
to receive the peace they seek? Be prepared with a stockpile of answers and reasons for your
faith. And if you're into stockpiling supplies too, well, I may be knocking on your door.

Prepare my heart and give me words, Lord, so I will know what to say to those who need hope.

ANTS

A little yeast works through the whole batch of dough.

GALATIANS 5:9

It happens every year in many American homes: Winter ends, and in its place, the warmth of spring arrives. Birds begin to sing, and kids go outdoors to play. It's all sunshine and tulips. And ants. They aren't noticeable at first, mind you. A single, tiny ant makes its way across the kitchen counter and you blame the hole in the screen door. You see a couple more the next day, but surely the crumbs on the floor are responsible for those. It doesn't seem like a big deal when you're removing one itsy-bitsy ant at a time.

Until, one morning, you walk into your kitchen for your morning coffee and find ants everywhere! Suddenly, you realize the problem is far more widespread than you thought. It doesn't take much for one ant to spread the word and invite all his ant friends to your kitchen for a party. Convincing these tiny invaders to leave can be very difficult once they've made themselves at home in your kitchen.

Sin works its way into our hearts in the same way a colony of ants works their way into a spice cabinet. It happens a little at a time. We lose our temper with our spouse and blame it on a bad night's sleep. A little gossip here and a bit of ungratefulness there, and we convince ourselves it's no big deal. The situation seems very manageable when it's just one indiscretion at a time.

Satan is sneakier than any annoying insect, and he won't be satisfied with a spiritual slipup every now and then. He won't stop until sin works its way into every area of our lives. He'll then seek to use our poor decisions to influence those around us. Before we know it, what once didn't seem like a big deal has totally overtaken us.

We must be proactive in protecting our hearts from the Enemy. We can ask God to reveal any hidden areas of sin before they overtake us (Psalm 139:24). Stopping a problem before it begins is much easier.

Help me remember that Satan doesn't try to tempt me in flashy ways; he's far more subtle. Reveal any secret areas of sin within me, Lord, so that they don't grow in my heart.

A COLD PLATE

They spoke against God, saying, "Can God spread a table in the wilderness?"

PSALM 78:19 ESV

Does your family ever stare into the pantry or refrigerator and declare that there's nothing to eat? Are you then able to look into the same pantry or refrigerator and pull together a tasty meal? You're probably able to do that because you did the shopping and you know what to look for. The key is to teach others what to look for. The next time your children insist there's nothing for lunch, there is something you can do.

Even when you're trying to make it to payday, you probably have everything you need to make a cold plate. This is a favorite in many homes. When the children stand in the kitchen and insist there's nothing to eat, proving otherwise is fun. A cold plate can be some applesauce, cheese, crackers, and mandarin oranges. Or dig up cottage cheese, pretzels, and carrots. Add some celery, raisins, or vanilla wafers; the options are endless. The next time your family doubts the contents of your pantry, whip up a cold plate and amaze them.

Time and time again, the Israelites doubted God's ability to take care of them. Often when they encountered hardship, they questioned God. They looked at their circumstances and were quick to declare that nothing good could be found. God looked at the same situation and saw it differently because He was the One who put them there, and He had good things in mind when He did it.

We've all done it. We've found ourselves struggling financially, navigating difficult relationships, or picking up the pieces of broken dreams. We've stood and stared and doubted that good could come from any of it. We forget that the God who fed His children in the wilderness is the same God who provides for us. He can spread a banquet table in the middle of the wilderness. He can produce an abundant crop in places where the Enemy can only plant seeds of doubt. We can trust Him when our options seem slim.

Lord, sometimes I'm tempted to look at my circumstances and think that nothing could come of them. Forgive me for the times I've doubted Your provision or Your plan for my life.

FINGERPRINTS
ON THE GLASS

*When they observed the boldness of Peter and John and realized that they were uneducated
and untrained men, they were amazed and recognized that they had been with Jesus.*

ACTS 4:13 HCSB

D o you have a technique for keeping fingerprints off of windows and glass doors?
What about bathroom mirrors, stainless steel refrigerators, and glass tabletops?
If so, please share because the only solution that some moms can think of is to lock
their children out of the house, and—let's be honest—that's generally frowned upon.

In all seriousness, some dish soap and hot water will do the trick. White vinegar
also works wonders to remove all evidence of little fingers on glass. Club soda is another
home remedy that is said to work.

Still, children tend to leave a mark wherever they go, whether a muddy shoeprint or
juice stains on the carpet. It's not their fault; children just have a way of making their
presence known.

Christ has a way of making His presence known as well. A person cannot come in
contact with the risen Savior and walk away unchanged. When we invite Him to change
us from the inside out, people will know that He's there. Others will sense Him in the
way we conduct ourselves, interact with others, and handle hardships. We'll leave fingerprints of grace everywhere we go. People will feel the love and know that we've been
with Christ. There will be something about us that sets us apart. Paul described it as
having "the marks of Jesus" on his body (Galatians 6:17).

As we go about our days, let's leave a few marks behind. Let's live in a way that lets
others know that we have been there (in a good way!).

*I don't want to slip through this life unnoticed, Lord. Help
me to leave marks of mercy and love everywhere I go.*

REDEEMING THE TIME

When they saw him from a distance, they could hardly recognize him; they began
to weep aloud, and they tore their robes and sprinkled dust on their heads.

JOB 2:12

Have you ever bumped into someone you hadn't seen in years and you barely recognized them? Have you seen someone after they endured a long illness and were shocked at how much they'd changed? Perhaps you yourself have gone through a stressful time and hardly recognize the person in the mirror these days.

Stress and grief can physically change a person. From dark circles under the eyes to brittle fingernails to a lowered immune system, trauma can make a person older from the inside out. The bright, shining demeanor you're accustomed to may have dimmed. When we connect with someone after they've endured a tragedy or loss and we think they look different, they probably do!

Job suffered unspeakable loss. His wealth. His health. All of his children. His friends heard of his dark days and came to be with him. As they approached his home, they saw him sitting in the dirt, and he was almost unrecognizable.

In the book of Ruth, Naomi had a similar story. She left her home country with her family. Tragedy struck, and she came home as a childless widow. As she entered her home town, the women all asked, "Can this be Naomi?" (Ruth 1:19). Grief had changed her physically so that the people were puzzled, and it changed her on the inside as she renamed herself "Mara," meaning *bitter* (v. 20).

Tragedy and trials change people. When it happens to someone around us, let's choose to walk with that person as they figure out what their new normal looks like. They probably won't be the same person they were before, and this may make us slightly uncomfortable. That's okay; let's get uncomfortable for them. God can redeem and restore, and we'll get the blessing of seeing them come out on the other side.

I'm so grateful that my pain doesn't make You uncomfortable, Lord. Thank You for walking with me through the darkest times.

RAINDROPS ON A WINDOW

God is faithful, who has called you into fellowship with his Son, Jesus Christ our Lord.

1 CORINTHIANS 1:9

Have you ever watched raindrops roll down a kitchen window? Everything viewed through the drops is a little distorted. Distances and sizes of objects seem to change. To watch the rain roll down and to observe the world through those drops is mesmerizing, but it's important to know that the view is inaccurate—much like trying to view God through the lens of pain or loneliness.

When we find ourselves in a painful place, we must remember that there are feelings and there are facts. They are both real, but they are not the same. We may feel lonely, but we are never alone. Things become distorted when we try to view our world through our feelings. Problems seem bigger, and He seems far away and smaller. We may feel like things are never going to change or get better. Everything seems wrong, and even God seems distant.

When we feel ourselves getting lost in loneliness, we must speak truth to ourselves. Our feeling of loneliness is not an indication that God is far away. Because God is faithful, we know that He is never aloof no matter what our feelings would have us believe. He is always within reach and close enough to hear the cries of our hearts.

When we need an accurate view of our God and our situation, let's remind ourselves of what we know to be true of Him. God is love (1 John 4:8), and He will never leave us (Deuteronomy 31:6). Let's take our eyes off of our circumstances and place them on our Savior.

Keep me in Your Word, Lord, so I will have an accurate view of You and a proper perspective when it comes to my problems.

THE GARAGE DOOR

"He will send out his angels with a loud trumpet call, and they will gather his elect from the four winds, from one end of heaven to the other."

MATTHEW 24:31 ESV

It's easy to know when a loved one is home if you have an attached garage. You can be sitting anywhere in your house and hear the familiar sound of the door opening. Sometimes the opener works from a distance: a person presses the button, but it may be a few minutes before they're in sight. If the person has been gone for some time, everyone has a chance to gather and prepare a proper welcome. The sound of a garage door opening can be the most beautiful sound when you've been waiting for someone you love to come home.

No one knows the hour or day when Christ will return (Matthew 24:36). We should be living in a way that we're always prepared to meet Him face-to-face. For now we should be meeting with Him each day through prayer, reading His Word, and worship. But as we wait, some believers will admit that they listen for the sound of a trumpet. The sound will surely be unmistakable even for those who aren't musically inclined.

No matter where on the earth you happen to be, the trumpet call will be heard by all. This long-awaited sound will let us know that our Love is returning. The excitement is almost too much. Scripture warns that some will say it's time when it is not. Their words might sound appealing to us, but they won't sound like a trumpet.

There are many beautiful sounds: a newborn baby's cry, waves crashing on the beach, raindrops falling through the trees, or the garage door when someone returns home. None of these sounds can compare to the sound of a loud trumpet call signaling Christ's return. That will be a glorious day!

You've created many beautiful sounds in the world, Lord, but I'm listening for the trumpet. Hasten the day when my faith becomes sight.

ROOM WITH A VIEW

There before me was a door standing open in heaven. And the voice I had first heard speaking to me like a trumpet said, "Come up here, and I will show you what must take place after this."

REVELATION 4:1

There is something about natural light that brightens a whole room. No amount of light bulbs can fill a room quite like sunshine streaming in through a window, leaving rays of light on the floor. Even better is a room where the windows offer a lovely view. To sit in a comfortable chair, sip some hot tea, and watch children play in the yard or a bird sit on a branch is such a peaceful way to pass the time. You just can't beat a room with a view.

Someone told a story long ago about an elderly woman who was bedridden. She could see only the exterior wall of a brick building when she looked out of her window. In order to make her smile, her son got permission to paint beautiful scenery on the brick wall. She would lie in bed and study the painting, and she could almost hear the rippling water in the brook and smell the flowers on the bank. The view made all the difference on the most difficult of days.

In the book of Revelation, we read about John's unprecedented view into heaven. He was permitted to glimpse the holy city, Jerusalem, and he described it as being bright as crystal (Revelation 21:10–11). He was able to see and take note of the walls, the gates, and the foundation of the city.

John had the unique privilege of being a part of Jesus' earthly life and seeing the Light of God in our world. How amazing that he was also able to look out and enjoy the view as well! How that view must have made all the difference on the hardest of days when he was persecuted and exiled.

We can have that same view. On the darkest of days, when we don't see the light pouring in, we can close our eyes and imagine the day when Jesus Himself will be our light (Revelation 21:23), and every room will have a view.

With You in my heart, Lord, I always have a room with a view.
Thank You for the light You shine on my path and into my heart.

FAKE FRUIT

The fruit of the Spirit is love, joy, peace, forbearance, kindness, goodness, faithfulness, gentleness and self-control.

GALATIANS 5:22–23

The first thing you would notice upon entering Blairanne's kitchen is the beautiful glass dish full of bright, yellow lemons. If you have spent much time on Pinterest, you have probably noticed that everyone seems to have this "fresh fruit in the kitchen" thing down pat. It's cheery, refreshing, and seemingly perfect. Perhaps you would be tempted to ask her how long those lemons will stay so pretty and yellow. She would tell you what she told me: "Forever, because they're fake."

As followers of Christ, there should be some fruit on display in our lives, and it should be real. People interacting with us should be able to see something refreshingly different. In this world where so many things are fake, people are watching to see if we are what we seem.

It is no light thing to call yourself a Christian. Christians are to walk as Christ walked and to love like He loved. People are hurting and struggling, and they'll look at our lives to see if Jesus has made a difference. If the fruit in our lives is all for show on Sunday morning, they'll lose their curiosity. If our fruit doesn't cause us to respond differently or treat others better, no one will be interested in the Christ we claim.

How can we know if our fruit is fake? We can ask ourselves a few questions. Do we only love people who love us back? Do we carry a grudge instead of grace? Does our peace turn into worry when things go wrong? Do we respond in kind instead of with kindness? Are we only generous if it isn't a sacrifice?

Let's be honest. Fake fruit has its charms. It's always pretty and easy to maintain, and if displayed properly, it impresses others. You just have to blow the dust off of it every now and then and everything is great.

But, when hard times come, a fake lemon won't take us very far. Similarly, the real fruits of the Spirit that come with sacrifice and sweat is what we, as Christ-followers, need to be offering to the world around us.

Help me to always remember that fake fruit is pretty
but it isn't beneficial. I want my fruit to be real, Lord, so
it will be refreshing to myself and those around me.

SMALL-TOWN LIVING

Whatever happens, conduct yourselves in a manner worthy of the gospel of Christ.
Then, whether I come and see you or only hear about you in my absence, I will know
that you stand firm in the one Spirit, striving together as one for the faith of the gospel.

PHILIPPIANS 1:27

If you've ever lived in a small town, you're aware that there are no secrets. Good or bad, everyone knows everyone's business. People are always watching, and they're going to talk. Having lived in towns of less than a thousand people for most of my life, I can tell you the trick to embracing small-town living. It's simple: be genuine and be yourself.

When you're always genuine, you don't have to worry about someone catching you doing something. If you pretend to be a perfect parent, you're going to be embarrassed when you get caught with a child having a meltdown in the grocery store. If you pretend to be someone you're not, then you have to remember who you're pretending to be and who you're with. Living that way is exhausting. It's much less stressful to simply be consistently genuine, and then it won't matter what folks see or say because they'll know the real you.

In Paul's letter to the Philippians, he advised them to consistently conduct themselves in a gospel-worthy manner. If any of them professed to be Christ-followers, people in the town were going to be watching. Whether Paul showed up unannounced to see them or the other folks in town sent word to him, Paul wanted them to be living genuinely because their lives were a reflection of Christ, who lived in them.

Christian living is much like small-town living. Folks are watching and they're talking; it's human nature to do so. If we're trying to feign perfection or put on a show, our charade won't end well. The goal is never perfection. The goal is a genuine life that, regardless of who's watching, points other people to Christ.

Lord, I want my life to honor You. I would rather be genuine and make mistakes than pretend to be perfect and be proven a liar. Help me to live a life worthy of the gospel of Christ.

HALF THE STORY

Now there are also many other things that Jesus did. Were every one of them to be written,
I suppose that the world itself could not contain the books that would be written.

JOHN 21:25 ESV

K ids love to be told stories. Being read a book at bedtime is great, but even better
is when Mom shares a personal story from her childhood. Most kids thor-
oughly enjoy stories about their parents' childhoods and things that happened long
before they were born. They love to hear what Dad was like at their age and want to
know all about his shenanigans. They're particularly interested in times when Mom
or Dad got into trouble, though most parents will keep the "best" stories to themselves! In many homes bedtime ends with children begging to hear more and parents
insisting that there just isn't enough time to share every detail of every story.

It's easy to view a person in one light and forget that people are multifaceted.
They can be fully one thing and also fully something else. If we focus on only one
side, we'll miss out on what makes that individual special. As we get to know more
and more about someone, we realize that there's still much we don't know, so we want
to know even more. One more story is never enough.

Even if you have a devotional time at some other point in the day, it's nice to read
yourself a bedtime story at night. There are many stories about Jesus throughout
the gospels that reveal His complexity. The narratives in Scripture give us glimpses
into His childhood and adulthood. We see humor, friendship, compassion, and
betrayal. We do well to remind ourselves that, while walking this earthly sod, He
was completely human. He cried real tears. He laughed out loud. He lost dear friends,
and He loved His mother. The opportunity to see this side of Jesus is a gift.

An essential part of Christianity is the understanding that Jesus was fully
God and fully man. We're given enough information to see both facets but also just

enough to know that there is so much we cannot know. Every story leaves us wanting more, and one more is never enough. Can you even imagine what stories John, the beloved disciple, chose to keep to himself? Maybe he'll tell us one more when we all get to heaven.

Someday, Lord, I'll get to hear all Your stories of healing and grace, and I just can't wait! I love Your story, and I'm so thankful that You wrote mine.

BLENDING IN

"Watch out for false prophets. They come to you in sheep's clothing, but inwardly they are ferocious wolves."

MATTHEW 7:15

Have you ever been guilty of slipping an ingredient that you knew someone didn't like into a dish you were preparing? Maybe you thought they wouldn't notice if it was disguised properly or would suddenly like the ingredient because of the way you prepared it.

One of the best ingredients to disguise in a dish is cream cheese. Lots of people think they dislike it and would turn their noses up were it offered on its own. The trick is to mix it with something that they do like. For instance, cream cheese mixed with some whipped topping makes a delicious dessert filling. Or mixed with salsa and shredded chicken, it makes an amazing enchilada. Cream cheese has the remarkable ability to blend in with a number of other ingredients until it's almost unrecognizable.

During the Sermon on the Mount, Jesus instructed His followers on a wide variety of issues. In that sermon Jesus warned them that false prophets would slip in among them. These individuals would blend in with the believers and might not be immediately recognizable. It was important that the church be on the lookout for such people, who were really wolves in sheep's clothing, intending to lead God's people astray.

This warning still applies to the church today. Certain people will offer us things that, on their own, we would never accept. But the Enemy is trickier than that, and he'll mix some undesirable things with things that aren't so bad. We're told that Satan disguises himself as an angel of light (2 Corinthians 11:14).

This doesn't mean we should be cynical or suspicious of people, but let's do be alert (1 Peter 5:8) as we go about our lives so that we're not fooled by evil in disguise.

I don't want to be cynical, Lord, but I don't want to be naive either. Give me wisdom and discernment as I go through life so I'm not led astray by evil in disguise.

HARDWOOD FLOORS

As for you, O man of God, flee these things. Pursue righteousness,
godliness, faith, love, steadfastness, gentleness.

1 TIMOTHY 6:11 ESV

Having hardwood floors in your home is a bit of a mixed blessing. They're certainly beautiful to look at and easier to clean than carpet. They give your home a look of elegance and increase its value. The downside to real hardwood floors is that they scratch very easily. One kitchen chair dragged or one dish dropped can leave scars that can't be removed.

More than one family has moved into a newly built home and immediately fallen in love with hardwood floors while they're still shiny, unblemished, and beautiful—only to discover that they lose their luster quickly. "Be gentle!" becomes a common refrain because Mom and Dad don't want to damage the floors.

Over and over in Scripture, God urges His children to be gentle with each other. People are beautiful, but we are also easily scarred. A misspoken word or an unkind act can leave marks that can't be removed. We've all encountered people who were not gentle with us, and we still remember how it felt.

When we receive the Holy Spirit and walk accordingly, one of our characteristics will be gentleness in our words, our actions, and our very spirit (1 Peter 3:4). This fruit of the Spirit should always be on display. In fact, our gentleness should be evident to everyone we meet (Philippians 4:5).

We don't want anyone to be more scarred after having met us. Even the strongest person among us needs kindness. Everyone has scars of some kind; some are more obvious than others. May our gentleness be a healing agent in their lives and direct them to the One who can heal every wound.

I never know when someone around me is having a hard time. Give me a gentle spirit, Lord. Let me be a soothing presence in the lives of others.

TASTE AND SEE

"But the Counselor, the Holy Spirit—the Father will send Him in My name—
will teach you all things and remind you of everything I have told you."

JOHN 14:26 HCSB

Bacon is a beautiful thing. We can all agree on that, right? You can't go wrong with a crispy slice with breakfast, chunks in your green beans, or bits in your salad. Bacon makes every dish better. It's an unfortunate moment when the last piece of bacon is consumed, but it doesn't have to be sad if you know how to make Ruby's fresh green beans.

Ruby was a firm believer that even if you don't have any bacon, you can have something to remind you of all of its goodness—because a good cook always saves bacon grease. The day after cooking bacon, Ruby warms the saved grease in a skillet until it melts. Then she cleans and snaps fresh green beans and drops them into a pot. Finally, she pours the wonderful, bacon-flavored, liquid love into the pot. Even though the bacon is gone, everyone can enjoy the aroma and flavor.

Jesus tried to prepare His disciples for the time when He would no longer be a physical presence in their lives. Simon Peter was distraught at the thought of not having Jesus physically with him. "Where are you going? . . . Why can't I follow you?" he asked (John 13:36–37). Jesus comforted them all by explaining that they didn't have to be sad when His last days on earth were complete.

They weren't going to physically have Christ any longer, but they would have Someone to remind them of Him and everything He had taught them. The Holy Spirit would come to them and bring the aroma and essence of Christ. Through the promised Spirit, the disciples would still have comfort and guidance after Jesus had physically departed.

Believers have the same gift today. We don't have Jesus physically with us, but we have all His power living in us. We can't touch Him but we can "taste and see that the LORD is good" because the Holy Spirit brings the aroma of Christ (Psalm 34:8). Let's ask the Holy Spirit to teach us "all things" and to remind us of Christ's teachings.

*I long for the day when I can physically see You, Lord,
but I'm thankful for the Holy Spirit, who reminds
me of Your power and presence in my life.*

STRAIGHT FROM
THE FRIDGE

As she stood behind him at his feet weeping, she began to wet his feet with her tears.
Then she wiped them with her hair, kissed them and poured perfume on them.

LUKE 7:38

Harold's home had a dining room. There were times when that's where he ate his meal. He would sit at the dining room table, eat off a nice plate, and mind his manners.

Other times, formality was tossed aside. There was no one to impress, and the only thing that mattered was the hunger. In those instances Harold would grab a fork, open up the refrigerator, and just pull up a chair. In the light of the fridge, Harold would sit and eat a pork chop sandwich straight from the fridge. There was no shame in my grandpa Harold's midnight snacking game.

Many people in Scripture interacted with Christ in a manner that was considered proper. There were certainly those who kept in line with all the expectations of the day. Perhaps some worshipped in the temple when He taught or waited for Him to call them to His side. There are certainly times when modesty and decorum are best.

But other times desperation trumps decorum. In those moments it doesn't matter what others may think or say. Some situations in life drive us to the feet of Jesus. During seasons of pain, we don't concern ourselves with the whispers or the stares of others. Everyone's journey to Jesus is different, and others may not grasp the magnitude of what it took for you to get there. That's okay. You can worship without shame.

You can cast yourself at Jesus' feet. You can raise your hands if the Spirit so leads. You can, like Paul, declare that you're unashamed of the gospel (Romans 1:16). You're unashamed of your Savior, and you will, if need be, cast yourself at His feet for all to see.

Sometimes, I get caught up in appearances, Lord. I worry what others may think about the way I love You. Give me boldness, Lord, to worship You with all that I am.

LANDLINE

For through him we both have access to the Father by one Spirit.

EPHESIANS 2:18

Do you remember when you had to remain attached to a wall in order to have a phone conversation? Your movement was limited to the length of your cord. The only way you could speak privately with someone was if you could stretch the cord long enough to close yourself in the hall closet. You could only speak with another person if she was at home and within earshot of her phone because it also was attached to a wall. Perhaps you even had to plan ahead for your phone call to be sure that everyone was in place.

How excited were you when you received your first cell phone? A whole new world was opened. You suddenly had the ability to call anyone at any time! You could talk to your girlfriend while shopping. You could call for help if you had car trouble. You could have a phone conversation while at home, at a restaurant, or in the restroom. (Don't pretend you haven't done it!) Don't we often take for granted this unrestricted mode of interacting with those around us?

At one time people had to remain in certain places in order to worship God. They had to be on a mountain, in Jerusalem, or at the temple. Worshippers had to lay out plans and make trips. There were restrictions and regulations regarding how one was to worship. A word from the Lord came through a prophet. Do you think they ever longed to just talk to God whenever they wanted to?

The presence of the Holy Spirit means that we have unrestricted access to the God of the universe. We don't have to be in a certain place. We don't have to plan ahead, and we won't have to have a third party relay the message for us. We have the privilege of talking to our heavenly Father whenever and wherever we want. A conversation can be had when we're alone or in a crowded room. He's listening on Sunday morning or in the dead of night. We can converse with Him anywhere.

Lord, I love knowing that I can speak to You
anytime and anywhere about anything.
If it matters to me then it matters to You.

FROM DARKNESS TO LIGHT

The people living in darkness have seen a great light; on those
living in the land of the shadow of death a light has dawned.

MATTHEW 4:16

Have you ever been in a room for so long that you didn't realize the sun had started to go down and the room had begun to darken? You're straining to read in a poorly lit area until your roommate opens the blinds or turns on a lamp, and you're amazed because you didn't realize how dark the room had become. Or you begin preparing supper in a brightly sunlit kitchen; after awhile, your husband comes home, asks you why you're working in the dark, and flips the light on. Suddenly, the room is bright, though you never realized you were cooking in the dark!

Life without Christ is a life lived in the dark. Perhaps moments of light stream into some days. Babies are born and good things happen. These are common graces that God gives to everyone like a rainbow after a storm. But often the respite is short-lived. The darkness will descend again, and many don't even know it. Some people go about their business every day without realizing they are living in the dark until Christ appears and shines His light.

The birth of Christ brought a bright light into a darkened land. Scripture says that the people were living in darkness. They were constantly in the shadow and never able to break out into the light. This had gone on for generations, and, chances are, many no longer even took note of the darkness.

Then, one day, a star shone in the East and announced that a great light had come into the world. Those who had been walking and stumbling around in the darkness saw the light and realized how dim their lives had been.

Who do you know who needs a light to shine on them? Who is trying to make their way through a poorly lit world? Point them to the Light of the World.

Thank You, Lord, for having compassion on Your people. I was lost and wandering in the dark before You came. I'm so thankful for Your light.

LOOKING IN THE WRONG PLACES

*Now all has been heard; here is the conclusion of the matter: Fear God
and keep his commandments, for this is the duty of all mankind.*

ECCLESIASTES 12:13

Do you ever wonder if, perhaps, things aren't as hard as we make them seem? Have you ever had a spouse or child (or yourself!) stare into a cabinet and declare that there aren't any clean plates? Most likely, the clean dishes are nestled safely in the dishwasher. But sometimes no one thinks to look there. It's easy to look so hard for something that you miss something seemingly obvious.

Many times in the book of Ecclesiastes, Solomon questioned the meaning of life. He searched for it in people, possessions, and pleasures. He questioned his existence and became frustrated by it all. Solomon was searching for purpose in all the wrong places, until he finally reached "the conclusion of the matter."

After all of his meditating, praying, and pondering, Solomon finally understood the whole duty of man: we are to fear God and obey Him. That seems like it should be pretty obvious, but it clearly isn't. We continually search for meaning apart from God through our jobs, our popularity, and our appearances. We look to our friends, our mentors, or our television sets to tell us why we're here. All along, Scripture tells us to keep God's commandments and then tells us exactly what those commandments entail.

There's no guesswork involved. All we need to do is open our Bibles and spend time in prayer, and He will reveal His purpose for our lives. Let's quit looking for love in all the wrong places when we can find it only in God.

Lord, I don't want to keep looking for meaning in things that don't matter. I will fulfill my duty by listening to and obeying You.

BIRD FEEDER

"The King will reply, 'Truly I tell you, whatever you did for one of the least of these brothers and sisters of mine, you did for me.'"

MATTHEW 25:40

Many people enjoy having bird feeders in their yards. Feeders offer a great way to interact with nature while giving birds access to food. Have you ever wondered what would happen to the birds if you didn't put a feeder in your yard? God would take care of them like He said He would (Matthew 10:29). God doesn't need us to feed the birds for Him, but isn't it fun to be a part of it all?

God doesn't need us in order for Him to do His work. He's perfectly capable of loving and caring for His creation. He loves every single person on this earth and will fulfill His purposes for each of them. Why, then, does He want us to feed the hungry? Why do we need to shelter the homeless or give clothing to those in need (Isaiah 58:7)? Why is it important for us to do any of these acts of service, knowing that God can take care of all of it without us?

We are to do these things out of obedience to God. We do them because the command to love our neighbor is one of the greatest (Mark 12:31). We learn to hold material possessions loosely and to view our fellow man as far more important than anything we can own. When we love others we are speaking the love language of Jesus.

We'll never regret putting some birdseed in a feeder once we see a redbird eat from it and fly away satisfied. Likewise, we'll never regret loving someone else by giving our time, our possessions, and our talents. We're invited to be God's hands in a broken world, and no matter how much we give away, we receive far more.

I'm privileged to be a part of the work You're doing, Lord.
Give me a generous spirit so that others may know You.

KITCHEN GADGETS

Search me, God, and know my heart; test me and know my concerns.

PSALM 139:23 HCSB

Handy dandy kitchen gadgets are available everywhere these days. There are devices to help us slice, dice, and purée our way to a fantastic feast. With minimal effort we can produce creations that wow our family and friends. Nevertheless, we can use every fancy electronic doodad we own and still fail to deliver what we intended. Do you know what will ruin an otherwise lovely meal? Serving undercooked meat will do it every time. It's okay; we've all done it.

You spread out your best tablecloth, and you even break out the fine china. The brussels sprouts are perfectly glazed, and the mashed potatoes are smooth and creamy. You snap a quick photo before sitting down because this meal is totally worthy of an Instagram post. You place the beautiful roasted chicken on an antique serving platter amid the oohs and ahhs of your family. Then someone cuts into that lovely bird, and you gasp in horror at the sight of pink, undercooked meat.

The threat of salmonella is certainly a dinner-party fail. All of the shiny culinary contraptions are nice, but sometimes an old-fashioned meat thermometer will do wonders of its own. The inside of the meat being properly prepared is far more important than the outside being pretty.

The world wants us to be obsessed with appearances. We're bombarded with companies telling us what to wear, how to fix our hair, and how to look younger than our age. Those of us with milestone birthdays coming at us like a freight train might be tempted to buy into the hype. We need to remind ourselves that none of it matters if our hearts are not right.

Let's examine our hearts daily. We can, like the psalmist, ask God to search us and reveal any areas where we may have wandered from Him. Let's ask God to check the condition of our hearts to ensure that they're properly prepared.

Forgive me, Lord, for sometimes focusing on
the outside and worrying about appearances.
Search my heart so that I'm pleasing in Your eyes.

PAST AND PRESENT

For if you turn back and cling to the remnant . . . know for certain that the LORD
your God will no longer drive out these nations before you, but they shall be a
snare and a trap for you, a whip on your sides and thorns in your eyes, until
you perish from off this good ground that the LORD your God has given you.

JOSHUA 23:12–13 ESV

There is something fascinating about what people choose to say at the end of their lives. Will they choose to admit some long-held secret? Perhaps they'll offer some final words of wisdom or reveal some long-hidden feelings. Some individuals, in those final moments, accept Christ. What might you say in those final moments?

One of the more interesting deathbed confessions was from a man named Christian Spurling. In 1934 people were obsessed with a monster that was reportedly spotted in Loch Ness. Sixty years after the Loch Ness monster sighting, a dying Spurling apparently revealed that it was all a hoax and that his stepfather was behind the whole thing. This confession probably failed to convince those who believed in the myth, but it's interesting, nonetheless.

Before Joshua passed, he gathered all the children of Israel and offered some final words to them. Joshua told them to let go of the past or they would be in danger of losing what God was giving them in the present.

It can be difficult to let go of the past. How often do we cling to the remnants of old relationships or old wounds? We find ourselves in a new place with good things, and still we look back. In Genesis Lot's wife attempted to cling to what was behind her, which didn't exactly turn out well for her (19:26).

It's important to remember the past but not cling to it. Let's be open to what God is doing in the here and now.

*Sometimes I'm tempted to live in the past
and to remember it as better than it was, Lord.
Help me to focus on where You have me now.*

FAMILY STYLE

God settles the solitary in a home.

Few things can compare with a nice dinner with all the trimmings, served up family style. A special bonding takes place when everyone sits around the same table and serves themselves from the same dishes of food. They share stories while passing rolls and solve problems over coffee and cobbler. Once you get used to eating family style, you'll never enjoy a TV tray on the couch again.

God never intended that anyone go through life alone. When Jesus sent the disciples out, He sent them out two by two (Mark 6:7). Even Moses, the man who spoke to God as a man would speak to his friend, did not do everything on his own. During the battle between Israel and Amalek, the Israelites only won when Moses' hands were lifted. When Moses could no longer hold his own arms up, Aaron and Hur each held an arm up (Exodus 17:12).

God has always had a heart for family. There are many familial descriptions in Scripture regarding God and His people. He is our Father and we are His children. Christ is the groom and we, as the church, are His bride. We are co-heirs with Christ (Romans 8:17), which is symbolic of how rights and property were passed down from one generation to another.

We have the privilege of helping to grow God's family, and we can begin by looking around us to see who does not have the luxury of a family style meal. There are lonely people all around us who need to be invited to pull up a chair. God places the lonely in families, and we should be open to the idea that He might have meant *our* family. Or perhaps we're the lonely ones with no table to gather around. We can ask God to give us those relationships. The beauty of the body of Christ is that anyone can be our brother or sister.

Let's gather around the table and break bread together.

Thank You for my family, Lord. Open my eyes to any who are lonely and need to be invited to our table.

WINDOWSILL

For God so loved the world that he gave his one and only Son, that
whoever believes in him shall not perish but have eternal life.

JOHN 3:16

What is currently sitting on your windowsill? For many of us, the windowsill holds a variety of things. There may be weeds that your child lovingly
picked and proudly delivered or a birthday card from a faraway friend. It might be
where you place your jewelry when you're baking, a child's artwork, or an item you
don't want to lose. The windowsill is where we display things we love, things we
are proud of, and things we want others to see. Don't we smile in satisfaction when
others take notice of the things we've proudly displayed?

If you've ever taken the time to enjoy a sunrise, a sunset, or a rainbow after a
storm, you recognize that God knows how to display the things He loves. Think
about snowcapped mountains, crashing waves, and all the wonders that God placed
in plain view for us to enjoy. God loves us immensely, and He proved it beyond a
shadow of a doubt by sending His one and only Son. When Jesus was baptized,
God spoke from heaven and declared, "This is my dearly loved Son, who brings me
great joy" (Matthew 17:5 NLT). You know He wanted us all to take notice. God's
pride in His Son and His love for us were displayed on the cross for all to see.

The cross was God's windowsill to display the One whom He loved, was proud
of, and desperately wanted us to see. Yes, the cross held suffering and had long
been a thing of shame. It's gruesome to imagine, but we can't look away because in
the brutality of the cross there is beauty to be seen. To fully grasp God's love for
us, we must fix our eyes on the marred face of our Savior and hear God say, "This
is my dearly loved Son on display for you."

We always put on display the things and people that we hold most dear. Thank You, God, for the beauty of the cross and for the love it displayed.

PICNIC

He said to them, "Go into all the world and preach the gospel to all creation."

MARK 16:15

What's your go-to dish when the summer heat has set in and the last thing you want to do is turn on the oven? It's probably something that requires little prep work and even less cleanup. The key here is that you want to be in the kitchen as little as possible. July and August should involve only cold cereal and bologna sandwiches; most cooks would be in agreement on that one.

One of the best options for meals during the summer is to pack up some of your favorite foods, gather some of your friends, and head outside. Being outdoors with a picnic lunch makes sweet tea taste a little sweeter and Grandma's macaroni salad taste that much better. Once you have one picnic, you'll be looking for reasons to go out and do it again all summer long.

In the same way, God never intended for us to sit in our comfortable, air-conditioned homes and hoard our faith. Christ left His home in heaven and brought hope and salvation to us, and He wants us to do the same.

There's a time for staying in, doing the prep work, and waiting. Every day is not necessarily the right time to have the gospel conversation; some moments are just ministry moments. We love on, serve, and listen to the people around us. Then, at the proper time, we have to be ready to pack up what we've been taught and take it out into the world.

Let's not be afraid to leave the comfort of our familiar surroundings. We can pack a little extra macaroni salad, invite our neighbors on a picnic, and tell them about the God who adores them.

My winter season, with me keeping to myself, has lasted too long. Here I am, Lord; send me out into all the world.

THE GATHERING PLACE

"Where two or three gather in my name, there am I with them."

MATTHEW 18:20

What room would you consider the heart of your home? For many people the kitchen is the default gathering place. We do the prep work, dish out culinary delights, and share stories in our kitchens as guests naturally gravitate around the island and barstools. You only have to watch any remodeling or home-purchasing show on television to see that open, spacious kitchens are in high demand.

If you've ever tried to make dinner with children underfoot, you understand. Children want to be where their parents are and vice versa. Sure, it makes a ten-minute job take twenty-five minutes. There will definitely be a spill of some sort, and the measurements may not be exact. The atmosphere is a little wild and crazy, but in most cases, we wouldn't have it any other way. We want to be with our people.

Jesus feels the same way about us. Whether at an event involving thousands or a husband and a wife praying together, He promises to be with His people. Whether in a church, a dorm room, a prison cell, or somebody's kitchen, Jesus will join His people wherever they are gathered.

We see this many times in Scripture. Jesus joined His apostles in the Upper Room, met His friends in the home of Mary and Martha, and, much to the dismay of the Pharisees of the day, sat with sinners in their own homes. Some days, He sat on a hillside with a picnic lunch. The gathering place was wherever Jesus' followers were at any given time. Just like our children are going to be wherever we are, Jesus will be wherever His people are gathered.

Jesus has made Himself easy for seeking souls to find. The heavy heart doesn't need to wonder if He's nearby. Jesus never hides Himself from those of us who love Him. He's closer than our next breath. He's nearer than our next heartbeat. He's right here with us. His favorite gathering place is in the hearts of His people.

I want to be wherever You are, Lord. Though I'd go anywhere to be with You, I'm so thankful that You chose the hearts of Your people as Your gathering place.

A CASSEROLE FOR EVERY OCCASION

*My dear brothers and sisters, take note of this: Everyone should be
quick to listen, slow to speak and slow to become angry.*

JAMES 1:19

A casserole can minister to people in a variety of situations. Did someone have a death in the family? Take a chicken casserole. Did someone have a baby? Go with a tater tot casserole. Is someone new in town? Leaving town? Did someone get a new job or lose a job? Are your friends having their home remodeled? Did Aunt Martha get bursitis in her elbow? There's a casserole for that.

A casserole is a universal symbol of comfort and compassion. It says, "I see what you're dealing with, so here's some food I covered in cream of mushroom soup just for you. Enjoy!" Personally delivering a casserole can speak volumes when we just don't know what to say. It can also prevent us from saying the wrong thing.

Many verses in Scripture caution against our tendency to speak too quickly or too often. We've all been there. We want to make someone feel better, so we begin talking. Our well-intentioned words aren't always well received. People need our presence far more than they need our words.

Be quick to listen. Hurting people need to be heard. They need to be able to voice their sorrows without interruptions. They need to cry without someone offering them a tired cliché. Healing can happen when people are free to feel the way they feel. We do not need to solve anything. We just need to show up. That takes the pressure off everyone involved.

The next time you're tempted to tell someone, "I know how you feel," preheat your oven instead. The next time you're about to say, "It's all going to be okay," break out your grandma's recipes. Let's face it, we rarely know how someone feels, and we can't guarantee that everything will be okay in the near future.

When words won't work, casseroles say it all.

Guard my tongue, Lord, when I'm tempted to speak just to fill the silence. Teach me the ministry of simply being present when someone is hurting.

GRANDPA'S TOOLBOX

His divine power has given us everything we need for a godly life through our knowledge of him who called us by his own glory and goodness.

2 PETER 1:3

No matter what you needed, it could be found in Grandpa's toolbox. A hand saw, a flashlight, or a pair of pliers? They were all in there organized by type, size, and likelihood of use. By simply making a trip to the big, red toolbox, Grandpa could fix just about anything. Wouldn't it be nice if Grandpa had a toolbox to fix fractured relationships and broken hearts? He may not, but God does.

Everything we need to live a godly life can be ours with the right kind of knowledge of God, and everything we need to know about God can be found in His Word. Do we need to know how we're supposed to handle loss, treat our enemies, or conduct business? It's in there. How are we supposed to love our neighbors, navigate disappointment, or be a friend? It can all be found in the pages of God's love letter to His people.

Within the pages of Scripture are all the tools needed to live the life we're called to live. We can study the life of Christ, see those tools in action, discover new tools to add to our toolboxes, and then pass it all on to our children. Our faith is the best tool we have, and we want it in the box our children inherit after we're gone.

John said that he could have no greater joy than to hear that his children were walking in the truth (3 John v. 4). He wanted to know his descendants were utilizing the tools he had left behind. It comes in handy to have Grandpa's toolbox in your garage, but it's even better to have the knowledge of God in your heart.

Thank You for the divine power that gives me everything I need to live a godly life. Teach me to use the tools well, Lord.

TOAST AND TEA

Kind words are like honey—sweet to the soul and healthy for the body.

PROVERBS 16:24 NLT

How do you handle being sick? Are you a tough-it-out kind of person, or do you stay in bed at the first sign of a sniffle? Nothing makes a person long for their mom quite like being ill. Every mom seems to have her own trick for making her family feel better that she probably learned from her mom. Depending on the particular malady, some old-fashioned remedies include warm lemon water, flat soda, or chewing on fennel seeds.

My mother was no different, and she had her own wonder-working combination. Any time we were feeling under the weather, she would serve up toast and tea. It soothed sore throats, calmed upset stomachs, and eased aching heads. The combination had a way of warming a person up from the inside out. There are certainly ailments that even a mom can't take away, but my mother's hot tea and buttered toast always seemed to bring a little bit of healing.

We've all had times when we've longed to ease the pain of a loved one. We struggle to decide what to do when we can't fix a situation with anything found in our kitchen. It may not even be a physical illness: hurts and losses of all types, wounds people can't see, and scars that go deep need antidotes. One of the best remedies in those instances can be a heaping dose of kindness.

Wounded people walk among us all the time. They hide their hurt behind pleasant smiles but on the inside are desperate for a little kindness in an often cruel world. What if we lavished kind words on everyone we came in contact with? What if we began being more generous with gracious words and more careful with critical ones?

We can't fix some situations, but we can use kind words to bring a little sweetness to the souls of those around us.

Guard my tongue, Lord. Help me speak words that bring sweetness and life to those around me.

FINDING QUIET TIME

"Be still, and know that I am God."

PSALM 46:10

We can all agree that life is pretty loud. Many noises constantly distract us. Have you ever sat down to pay bills and been interrupted so many times that you just gave up? Or perhaps you've gone all the way upstairs but forgot why you were there because you were stopped on the way. Phones ring, clothes dryers buzz, dishwashers hum, kids cry, and dogs bark. Noise is everywhere!

The noises that heap stress on our souls don't consist of the day-to-day sounds of life but of the anger on the Internet, the drama constantly unfolding on the news, and the discord in church pews. Neighbors who just can't get along, the people who refuse to forgive, and the constant need to judge and compare—all of these things become incessant noise.

What's the answer to turning down some of the unnecessary noise in our heads and hearts so we can better hear from God? For one, we can choose better background noise. Whether you're a retiree or a stay-at-home parent, you probably want a little sound in the house, and the default tool is often the television. The TV can be full of negative emotions and scenarios. Perhaps we could choose to listen to a podcast, music, or audiobook.

Sometimes, the loudest noise is inside our own heads. We, like Martha, are anxious and troubled about so many things (Luke 10:41). Jesus didn't say that Mary didn't have things which could have caused her to feel troubled. The difference was that Mary chose the better thing to focus on: Jesus. Let's also choose worship over worry.

Whether our days are full of staff meetings, business lunches, play dates, or doctor's appointments, we can still end on a quiet note. We can take a deep breath, read a little, and laugh with someone. We can thank God for the people He's placed in our lives, drink a little something hot, and dream about tomorrow. If we're not intentionally seeking some quiet, the negative noises will take over.

What do you do to add a little peace and quiet to your day?

Teach me to filter out the negative noises in my day,
Lord, so that I'm better positioned to hear Your voice.

LOVE YOUR NEIGHBOR

"The second is this: 'Love your neighbor as yourself.'
There is no commandment greater than these."

MARK 12:31

If you've ever had the driver in front of you purchase your coffee at a drive-through or discovered that someone had already picked up your tab at a restaurant, you know how good it feels to be the recipient of someone's generosity. Random acts of kindness are certainly wonderful to receive and even more wonderful to perform. The thing is that these acts are, by nature, random. We may or may not know the person on the other end of our kind deed.

One family instituted a "Love Thy Neighbor" project in an attempt to be intentional about loving those around them. They asked God to open their eyes and hearts to needs in their community. They chose someone each month to love on through a homemade gift or some act of service. One morning they stood at the end of the driveway with donuts and coffee for the trash men. Another day they walked into a local nursing home and asked, "What can we do to brighten the day for those who live here?" The goal behind each act was that someone, in that moment, would feel loved.

When Jesus says, "There is no commandment greater than these," we should probably take note. The parable of the Good Samaritan tells us a little more about how Jesus intended this loving-your-neighbor thing to play out (Luke 10:29–37). The one who loved his neighbor interrupted his own plans to help someone else. He stopped, bandaged wounds, and showed mercy. He took time and got his hands dirty. That's what it looks like when we love our neighbors.

Random acts of kindness are a blessing, so we need not say, "No, thank you," to a free cup of coffee. But is it possible that we're called to something more? Something more intentional? Something that makes us uncomfortable? Something that isn't quite so sanitary? Let's be intentional in our love for others.

Forgive me, Lord, for the times I've passed my neighbor by in their time of need. Help me do the hard work of loving people well.

THE WISHBONE

He said to them, "This kind cannot be driven out by anything but prayer."

MARK 9:29 ESV

Raise your hand if you and your siblings ever waited in anticipation for the Thanksgiving turkey to be carved just so you could have the wishbone. Many sets of siblings have stood face-to-face, each with a firm grasp on the bone, and pulled with all their might in hopes of having a wish granted. Unfortunately, a wishbone winner has never turned into a princess or woken up to a pony, because the bone of a turkey does not, in fact, hold any wish-granting powers.

We spend precious time and energy wishing things were different. We can lose ourselves in all of the what-if scenarios and trying to figure out what can be done to change our situations. The fact is that there are things in our lives that can't be wished, worked, or worried away. Some things are only driven out by the power of prayer.

In the gospel of Mark, we read a story about a father whose son was demon-possessed. He brought the boy to the disciples, but they were unable to cast the demon out. They had been given the power to heal disease, so what was the problem? When asked, Jesus informed them that some things are only driven out by prayer.

We have the power of the One who conquered death living in us, and yet we still attempt to handle things on our own. We act as if we can make things better by working just a little bit harder. Why do we do that? When something seems too much for us to handle, let's not waste our time wishing. Let's use the power of prayer to change our circumstances.

You can handle everything I encounter, Lord. I'll be a woman of prayer, and I'll turn to You in every situation.

ARE WE THERE YET?

*"Calling ten of his servants, he gave them ten minas, and
said to them, 'Engage in business until I come.'"*

LUKE 19:13 ESV

If you've ever been on a road trip with your children you know that, within five minutes of leaving the driveway, someone will ask the dreaded question: *Are we there yet?* People hold different philosophies on answering this one. Some will say, "Almost," in an attempt to smooth things over. Others go for brutal honesty and answer, "No, we're still far, far away."

Some parents go with the middle-ground answer: "It won't be long." The trouble with this mollification is that once children believe their destination is within reach, they stare out the window, expecting to see Granny's house around every turn. They miss the beauty of the journey because they're focused on the destination.

On the other hand, when children understand that they're nowhere near their grandparents' house, most will find things to do. They'll watch a movie, read a book, make up games, or eat a snack. They enjoy the journey much more.

Do you ever look at what's going on in the world around you, look to the skies, and ask, "Are we there yet?" It seems like people have been saying that Jesus is coming back any day for a very long time. It's possible that believers have been saying that ever since He left. We long for that day and, therefore, are constantly looking for it.

In the book of Luke, Jesus told a parable about a nobleman who was going to a far country. He gathered ten of his servants and gave them each some money with one instruction. He did not say to stand in the doorway, stare off into the distance, and look for his return. He did not say to look for signs or study the skies in an attempt to guess when he would return. The instruction was to work. For how long? Until he returned. That was all the information his servants needed.

Are we there yet? We could, with the best of intentions, say, "Almost." The truth, however, is that nobody knows. Perhaps we should stop spending so much time staring at the skies and simply work until He comes.

There are many things that could become distractions, Lord. Help me to focus on the journey and work diligently until You come.

COVERED IN CHOCOLATE

Above all, love each other deeply, because love covers over a multitude of sins.

1 PETER 4:8

You could cover any food in chocolate, and somebody would eat it. The food blogger Pioneer Woman won many hearts when she covered potato chips in chocolate! Shoppers can find raw onions covered in chocolate in candy shops in Philadelphia. Apparently, chocolate-covered pickles are a thing, as are an assortment of chocolate-covered bugs. (It takes all kinds.)

You just never know when you'll need to coat something in chocolate. Whether you start with something salty, sweet, or spicy, chocolate makes everything better. Who knows how many new desserts have been developed because someone made a mistake and thought, *What if I just cover it in chocolate?*

In his letter to fellow believers, Peter gave several instructions. The believers were to exhibit self-control and to be sober-minded. Yet, in 1 Peter 4:8, he advised them to put one thing above all else in their daily lives. "Above all, love each other deeply, because love covers over a multitude of sins."

Shallow love causes us to be easily offended and slow to forgive. Imagine if our Savior loved us that way! What if He held every offense against us indefinitely? We don't have to worry because, when Jesus loves, He loves extravagantly. His love led Him straight to the cross. Love just doesn't get much deeper than that.

Let's choose to love lavishly. Grace should ooze out of us like the melted chocolate inside a molten lava cake. Let's love deeply. Then we'll be able to seek and grant forgiveness faster and get back to the business of living for Christ and sharing the gospel. Who knows how many relationships could be restored if someone thought, *What if I just cover it in love?*

Teach me, Lord, to love like You love. When I'm tempted to hold a grudge or cling to an offense, help me to cover it all in love.

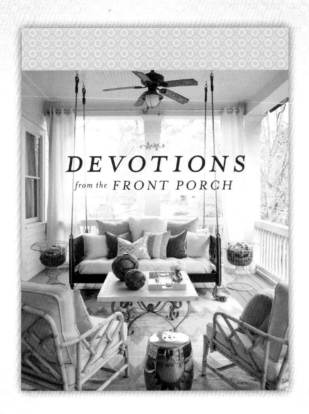

DEVOTIONS
from the **FRONT PORCH**

Let the peace of God lift your soul as you experience powerful devotions from your favorite places. *Devotions for the Beach*, *Devotions from the Garden*, and *Devotions from the Front Porch* will remind you of God's constant presence and bring inspiration to your daily life.